TAKE OFF
the cape

FROM SUPERHERO
TO SUPER COACH

MIDJA FISHER

Editing: fullstoppublishing.com.au
Cover: fostercreative.co
Layout & Production: smartwomenpublish.com

Table of Contents

Part 1: DISCOVER

Part 2: REVEAL

Part 3: EMPOWER

Dedication

For Tom, Sophie and Jack,

who inspire me to do more and be more

About Midja

Midja Fisher is an expert in creating confident leaders. She inspires people to step up and lead with courage and authenticity. She is a dynamic speaker and facilitator who shares her experience and stories openly and passionately.

Midja is a trusted mentor who helps leaders develop their own leadership style and increase their industry presence. She motivates others to discover their purpose, realise their talents and focus on what truly matters most. She is the author of two previous books, *Unshakeable Confidence* and *Great Lawyer to Great Leader*.

Midja's background includes 20 years' experience in the corporate world as a partner of a national law firm, and a learning and development specialist. Midja has a double degree in law and information technology. She's worked extensively throughout Australia in many different industries, with clients such as Queensland Law Society, WSP, North Queensland Toyota Cowboys, PKF Australia Accountants, Ashurst, RSL Queensland, and many more.

What's unique about Midja is her infectious energy, enthusiasm and optimism. With her blend of empathy and conviction, Midja challenges her clients to step out of their comfort zones to see what is possible.

Midja lives on the sunny Gold Coast with her three children and her cavoodle. She adores the sunshine, a glass of champagne and being in or on the water.

You can get in touch with Midja at www.midja.com.au.

Acknowledgements

I've been fortunate in my career to have been nurtured and empowered by a group of incredible leaders – just the best! A huge heartfelt thank you to all of you for your advice, wisdom and encouragement.

Special thanks to the group of amazing professionals who helped me put this book together, from editing, designing and publishing, to photographing and styling – Lauren Shay, Bev Ryan, Melinda Hird and Sylvie Velt. (It takes a village!)

To my tribe of gorgeous girlfriends, thank you for sharing this ride with me. I love hanging out with you guys – the stories, the laughter, the champagne! Life's so much better with you by my side. Here's to many more adventures together.

To my clients, thank you for the privilege of working with you and the opportunity to share my experiences and knowledge. You make my worklife an absolute joy. I'm always learning and growing from our time together and I look forward to sharing this book with you.

To my incredible family – Rell, Tom, Sophie and Jack. Your love and support keep me striving to do more and be more. Love you like crazy!

And finally, to you, thank you for reading this book. My hope is that it inspires you to lead your team with confidence and authenticity. I want you to fall in love with leadership and realise the magic you can bring to your team and organisation.

Midja x

Introduction

Introduction

WHO DOESN'T LOVE A SUPERHERO?

I mean, the cape, the mysterious mask, the secret identity, the superpowers … not to mention the praise and adulation. What's not to love?

The word "superhero" dates back to at least 1917.[1] The first superheroes included mythical characters and gods, such as Odysseus and Heracles, as well as folk heroes like Robin Hood. In the 1960s, Marvel Comics brought together the biggest assortment of superheroes into publication, including the famous characters

---

[1] "Superhero", Wiki 2. https://wiki2.org/en/Superhero

of Spider-Man, the Hulk, Iron Man, Thor, Daredevil and Captain America, just to name a few.[2]

Fast-forward to the present, and Hollywood is making big money creating movies centred on our favourite superheroes. *Aquaman* (2018) grossed $U1.15 billion, *Ironman 3* (2013) $1.21 billion, and the final instalment in the Avengers series, *Endgame* (2019), grossed a whopping $US2.8 billion – the highest-grossing film of any type of all time![3]

It seems we all love a superhero story, but why?

Maybe we love the fact that the hero has had to overcome adversity through hard work and determination. Maybe it's the action-packed pace of the story, with wizardry special effects bringing fantasy to life. Maybe it's something to do with the superhero's secret identity; think Bruce Wayne, Clark Kent and Peter Parker – people who carry on with their "normal" lives until they're called to action and transform into their superhero alter ego.

Whatever the reason, we idealise these superheroes and see them as unique, talented individuals who save the day. The superhero is often an outcast who has acquired unique powers at birth or through some accident or gift. They're revered and adored for their heroism.

But what happens when you try to become the superhero of your team? When you put on your cape and fly through the office doors to save the day and rescue your people?

---

[2] "Superhero", Wikipedia. https://en.wikipedia.org/wiki/Superhero
[3] Bajgrowicz, B. "The 10 Highest-Grossing Superhero Films Of All Time (According To Box Office Mojo)", 1 January, 2020. https://screenrant.com/highest-grossing-superhero-films-box-office-mojo

Unfortunately, you may not experience the happy ending of the Hollywood blockbusters we love to watch.

As a leader, I've tried to be the superhero and wore my cape proudly. I've tried my best to protect my team and rescue them from imminent danger: unrealistic deadlines, client complaints, and demanding executives. But for me, it was exhausting and unsustainable.

Now, I hear the same story from my clients – clients who are trying to navigate their role as leaders, juggling competing interests. Sound familiar?

Maybe you, too, are a leader who is trying to do the right thing for yourself, your people, your clients and your organisation. You're attempting to be everything to everyone and trying to save the day, every day. It's busy, and you're pulled in so many different directions.

You're smart, great at what you do, and you care about your team. You want to achieve great things and be a leader people want to follow. Yet, perhaps you're missing something. Maybe you need a different perspective, a deeper level of self-awareness, a mindset shift or some practical strategies to step up and lead your team with confidence and courage.

This book is for you. It's a book for anyone who wants to take off the cape, hang up the mask, and put down their weapon. It's for leaders who want to empower their people and see them succeed; leaders who, instead of playing the superhero, want to be the super coach.

Happy reading.
Midja x

Introducing the Superhero Leader

Introducing the Superhero Leader

"DO YOU WEAR YOUR UNDIES ON THE OUTSIDE?"

I asked one of my mentoring clients this question recently. She tilted her head and looked at me strangely. "What do you mean?" she asked. I explained the concept of the superhero leader: the person in the office who swoops in to save the day. She laughed and nodded. I laughed, too. I've been the superhero leader myself.

Modelling your leadership style on a superhero isn't all bad. Let's take a look at some of the positive characteristics of superheroes:

- Extraordinary powers and abilities
- A strong moral code
- Confidence and courage
- A great sense of responsibility

That doesn't sound like a bad leader, does it?

We *want* leaders who are driven, confident and have strong morals. The problem is when leaders try to be everything for everyone. The motivation behind the superhero's actions and their impact can lead to an ineffective workplace, where the leader and their team don't work to their full potential.

WHAT MOTIVATES THE SUPERHERO LEADER?

As the superhero leader, you have the best of intentions. You want to be there for your people and support them in their times of need. You want to protect and rescue them. You don't want to see them struggle or get something wrong.

You also want to achieve the best results for your clients. You've been doing this type of work for a long time, and you know what works. No one knows more about this work than you. You can't help but step in and take over when you know it's going to mean a better result for the client. It's about wanting to maintain the reputation of your team and organisation, and doing the right thing for the client.

As a leader, you're busy all the time. You juggle a never-ending to-do list, deal with competing priorities, and things need to get done quickly. Naturally, you want to go for the quick win, which means getting in there and doing things yourself. It just seems the easiest way. You know what works best, you've done it millions of times before, so it makes sense for you to take over and do it. Efficiency at its best.

Maybe being the superhero leader is a little about your ego, too. You love the sense of being the rescuer, the one who is needed and indispensable. Just like the superheroes in our favourite movies, you want to feel good about yourself. You crave the applause, the reward, and to be seen in a particular way.

You may also love the sense of urgency that comes from a crisis. It can be addictive. The immediacy and importance of being a superhero leader can make you feel alive. And even if there isn't a crisis, no problem – you can always create one.

Leading as a superhero may have become a habit; your default leadership style. It's the only way you know how to add value. The fact is that most of us don't become a leader unless we're extremely good at our technical work. We've been the expert in our field, which is why we've been asked to step up into a leadership position. It can be hard for us to let go of the "doing".

Being a superhero leader becomes your identity. You wear the cape because it feels easy, safe, and comfortable. But what's the impact?

IMPACT ON YOU

As the superhero, you fall into the habit of rescuing your people. You tend to get involved in the details of a project and micromanage. You see your people as dependant on you to get the job done, and they probably are. You've trained them well.

When times are great and results are achieved, you're congratulated and revered by your people. They love you and look up to you. It feels great.

But when times are tough, watch out. Your people have no accountability, which means the blame game will be fiercely played. If you're the one making all the calls, when things go badly (and in business, they do from time to time), you'll be the one to blame. Can you believe it, after everything you have done for your people? This makes you resentful and angry. You work long hours in the office doing your work *and* theirs. You start to feel like everyone is taking advantage of you.

Being the superhero also means you don't have time to stretch and grow. You're stuck solving problems that should be the responsibility of your people, so your career stagnates.

And you're tired. You feel like you're always in demand. You can never seem to find the time to think strategically and focus on the things that matter most. You're stuck playing small.

How long can you successfully play the superhero? Is it a sustainable role?

IMPACT ON YOUR PEOPLE

When people are led by a superhero, they feel safe and protected. They know their superhero will be there for them whenever they need them, day or night.

It's like living in Gotham City and putting out the bat signal. All people need to do is sit back and wait for Batman to arrive and save the day. And guess what? He always does.

This is comforting for your team, but it creates many negative impacts.

When your people rely on you to rescue them, they stay dependant. They never move through the critical stages of independence and interdependence. Their growth and development are stifled. They don't have to think for themselves because they know you are there to solve their problems. They develop learned helplessness.

There's also no accountability or responsibly in this type of work environment. People feel like the victim. They feel helpless, so all they can do is wait for you to make the decisions. In every meeting, they defer to you – a bunch of "yes" people agreeing with you.

"If two people have the same opinion, one is unnecessary."

- DR STEPHEN COVEY

A team with a superhero leader is full of people who don't know how to think for themselves. There's no creativity, initiative, or problem solving.

People start to believe they aren't capable of solving their problems. They question their ideas and judgement, and say to their clients, "I'll just have to check with my manager." A superhero leader keeps them playing small.

Eventually, your most engaged and driven team members will leave. The type of working environment you have created might be tolerable for the short term, but anyone who wants to grow, learn and be challenged will not want to stay.

Only the ones who are happy to do as little as possible will remain. They want to play small, and may even take advantage of your superhero leadership style.

IMPACT ON YOUR ORGANISATION AND CLIENTS

Ultimately, your organisation and your clients will suffer enormously.

No one – not you and certainly not your team – is working to their full potential or adding value. No one is happy or motivated. There's no excitement, no opportunity for growth and development, no innovation or creativity.

The result is high staff turnover, client dissatisfaction, and less-than-impressive financial results. Something must change, and it starts at the top with leadership.

There is another way to lead. Instead of being the superhero, you can be the super coach!

WHY IT'S TIME TO TAKE OFF THE CAPE

At the time of writing this book, I'm working from home. We all are. I'm home schooling my children, coaching my clients via Zoom, and enjoying the quiet time. But I also deeply miss the much-loved social interaction I usually have with my friends, extended family and work colleagues.

We're in the midst of a global pandemic: COVID-19, the effects of which we will feel for a long time.

Even before this pandemic, we were experiencing a time of rapid change. But this global crisis has well and truly confirmed the fact that we're living in a time of unprecedented uncertainty. The world is transforming, and the business landscape is evolving rapidly.

Challenging times are ahead for leaders, but so, too, are great opportunities.

"In the midst of chaos, there is also opportunity."

– SUN TZU

Technology is making it easier for us to work anywhere, any time. Sounds great, doesn't it? Yet this technology also means we're constantly accessible. We're always on, 24-7.

The race is on for businesses to automate more of their processes and leverage technology to produce more for less. There is constant pressure to cut costs and produce company growth for shareholders. Companies try to carefully balance this pressure for growth with their ethical responsibilities, which have been highlighted over the past few years.

In 2018, we saw the Banking Royal Commission. I think we all knew that banks weren't perfect, but most of us were shocked by the scale of bad behaviour across the financial sector. The Royal Commission revealed that the financial industry had been ripping off all kinds of people, even the dead, in the name of profit and fattening their bottom lines. It truly was a culture of profit before people.

Investigations into elder abuse and neglect were also made through the Royal Commission into Aged Care Quality and Safety. Once again, the spotlight shone on an industry that made decisions around profit, processes and ethics.

Through all of this, we have seen a push for businesses to drive sustainability and optimise their financial, social and environmental impacts. Quite a juggling act. We're told that sustainability in business is not only good for the planet, but it can also be a strong value driver and promote innovation.

Basically, a lot is going on! We live in a world of rapid social, technological and economic change. In response, our business models and structures are also shifting.

The question is, can all these priorities be balanced?

LET'S TALK ABOUT YOUR CLIENTS

Every day, your clients interact with the world's leading digital businesses. Think Uber, Amazon and Apple. These businesses set client expectations across the board. The question I want to ask you is, how do you measure up?

Your clients know what they want and aren't afraid to demand it. Businesses need to meet and exceed these high expectations to gain client loyalty and market share.

There has been a power shift from business to client. Clients are now more informed and resourced, and they are well-positioned to drive their own agenda.

Your clients' businesses have also become more complex, and so, too, have their business problems. They're dealing with their own rapid technological changes, high volumes of data, pricing pressures and regulation challenges. Their world is changing, and they need you to keep up. They need you to listen and understand their unique problems.

As a leader, you need to deliver a quality service to your clients and produce exceptional outcomes to gain their trust and loyalty. You need a talented, dedicated group of people in your team to make this happen.

WHAT ABOUT YOUR PEOPLE?

Amid all this change and uncertainty, your people have their own needs and wants in the workplace. They're struggling with their problems and look to you as their leader for help.

Research finds that workers in Australia and New Zealand have lacklustre employee engagement scores. Only 14% of workers are engaged in their job and show up each day with the enthusiasm and motivation to be highly productive. Another 15% of employees are actively disengaged. They're not only unhappy at work but also determined to undermine their colleagues' positive efforts. The remaining 71% of employees fall into the "not engaged" category. They show up every day to work, but they only do what is necessary and no more.[4]

Hmm. There's a lot of room for improvement here, and some work for us to do as leaders. Remember, it's your job to understand and meet your peoples' expectations. (Hey, no one said leadership was easy!)

---

[4]   *State of the Global Workplace*, Gallup, 2017. https://www.gallup.com/workplace/238079/state-global-workplace-2017.aspx

SO, WHAT DO YOUR PEOPLE WANT?

Safety

It's hard for your people to do their best work when they're worried, stressed or afraid. They might be afraid of failing, stressed about their workload, or worried about losing their jobs. Most people seem to have been made redundant at least once in their career, or their partner has. The impacts of this make people feel cautious and afraid.

We no longer consider disposable shopping bags, takeaway coffee cups or plastic straws acceptable. So, why is it still acceptable in business to have disposable employees?

When the numbers don't add up, leaders can be quick to dispose of their people as a first priority. How can anyone perform at their best if they believe that at any time, they could get a tap on the shoulder and be told they're out?

With the uncertainty and busyness of life, your people want safety. They want their work to be what I call one of the "secure tent pegs" of their life.

You see, I think life is a lot like pitching a tent in a campground. To secure it you need to have a certain number of tent pegs in the ground. To feel secure in life, you need to have some areas of permanency: your work, partner, family, friendships, health and home.

Without enough tent pegs fixed securely in the ground, you're vulnerable. Your tent could fly away with the next gust of wind, or rain could seep in, and you end up wet, cold and miserable. Not much fun!

As a leader, you're in charge of one of your people's tent pegs – their work. It's up to you to make that peg as secure as you can, to make your people feel safe.

Direction

Your people want a clear sense of direction. They want to know where the business is going and how they can contribute. They want to know the outcomes they're responsible for and how they will be measured – the blueprint for success in their role. They want simplicity and clarity. They want certainty in an uncertain world.

Your people lead busy lives. Countless priorities and people pull them in different directions. No one has the time to waste on things that don't matter. Your people must understand their priorities at work, and spend their time on what matters most. Nothing is more frustrating than working on something that ends up being disregarded and filed away with no discernible outcome. It's demotivating and disengaging.

Everyone in your team wants to move in the same direction, towards a common set of goals. They want to align with and contribute to the bigger picture.

Purpose

Everyone wants to do meaningful work – work that matters. How can your people turn up to work fully engaged every day if they don't feel that what they do makes a difference? Your people want to use their skills to make some kind of contribution.

Simon Sinek's famous TED Talk, "Start with Why," and his book of the same name sparked the increasing desire for people to understand why they go to work every day. People now focus not only on their job title (what they do) but on their *why* – why they do what they do.

Sense of belonging

Now more than ever, people look to their work and organisations for a sense of belonging. This desire to feel connected to others is intuitive. Your people want to feel part of something bigger than themselves. They want to be part of a tribe.

"We may have left traditional tribal settings back in the deserts but the instinct to tribe is still strong."

– MICHAEL HENDERSON

People once gained this sense of belonging from their church, extended family, or community groups. But, as many of us no longer have these close ties in our lives, we look to our workplaces to fulfil this need.

Your people want to fit in. They want to feel connected to their organisation, their leader, their fellow team members, and the work they do every day.

Recognition and opportunity

Finally, your people want to be seen, heard and recognised for their contribution. The type of recognition they seek might be different, but everyone wants to know that what they do matters. There is nothing more rewarding than having your hard work noticed, and nothing more demotivating than feeling as though you're invisible.

Your people want to receive useful feedback that recognises their strengths and allows them to grow in the areas they need to develop. They want the type of feedback that makes them know you care about them and that you want them to succeed. They want you to believe in them and give them the opportunity to learn and grow in their role.

OK, SO WHAT DOES ALL THIS MEAN FOR YOU, THE LEADER?

For you to thrive as a leader in this time, it's time to take off the cape.

The leaders who will come out on top and flourish are those who are open to new ways of inspiring and influencing their people. They're leaders who embrace collaboration and innovation. You have the opportunity to respond to this new world; to step up in your leadership role and adapt to the needs of your clients and your people.

Unfortunately, the superhero leader doesn't have the mindset or skillset to meet all these needs. Yes, they may be able to make people feel a certain level of safety and belonging, but it comes at a cost: a high level of dependency and little sense of purpose and recognition. It's all about the superhero, and without their superhero, people are lost.

Our businesses need a different kind of leader – one who understands the art of listening and questioning, who has creativity, empathy, compassion, and human intelligence. A leader who gives their people a sense of belonging and value.

The super coach.

The super coach motivates, inspires, and empowers their people. They drive positive change and innovation, making the most of the opportunities that changing technology presents. They leverage this technology to serve their clients and help their people to work smarter, not harder.

This super coach is YOU!

You're a leader who wants to inspire, create connection, and gain the trust and commitment of your people. You want to make a difference in their lives, and your clients' lives.

So, let's talk about how we can make that happen.

BECOMING A SUPER COACH

Great leaders are great coaches; in fact, they're super coaches!

A super coach inspires their people to develop to their fullest potential and significantly improve their performance. They embrace collaboration and innovation in the workplace. They lead their people by balancing confidence and humility. They share a strong message, yet also listen empathically. Most of all, they believe in their people.

One of my favourite descriptions of leadership is this one by Stephen Covey:

"Leadership is communicating others' worth and potential so clearly that they come to see it in themselves."

The superhero vs the super coach

THE SUPERHERO	THE SUPER COACH
Rescues their people	Educates, mentors, trains and coaches their people
Has all the right answers	Has all the right questions
Stoic	Vulnerable
Competitive	Collaborative
Focusses on their success	Focusses on the team's success
Confidence from the cape	Confidence from within
Tells	Listens
Paradigm of scarcity	Paradigm of abundance

Transforming from a superhero to a super coach means thinking and acting differently. If you've been the superhero of the office for a long time, it can seem a little daunting to change how you lead. Your superhero role is well known and well rehearsed. You slip that cape on every day without even thinking about it.

The role of the super coach is to educate, mentor, train and coach their people to their highest potential. It's all about focussing on the team's results, having the confidence to ask questions, listening to understand your people, and having the courage to be vulnerable.

Tough? Yes.

Worth it? Absolutely.

TYPE OF LEADER	OBSTACLE	ACTION TO TAKE	LEADERSHIP CAPABILITY
Super coach	Balance	Expand	100%
Coach	Trust	Leverage	70%
Superhero	Confidence	Self-awareness	50%
Sidekick	Experience	Develop	20%
Unknown hero	Presence	Build	10%

Unknown hero

The unknown hero is starting their career. There is so much to learn that they can feel overwhelmed at times. They're yet to build their reputation and make their mark as a leader. They are largely unseen in the organisation. The unknown hero may feel like they're working hard but not achieving anything. They lack **PRESENCE** and influence, and are unsure of their leadership capability or even if they want to step up into a leadership role. They need to start to **BUILD** their brand, find their voice, be seen, and learn as much as they can.

The sidekick

The sidekick is ready to become a leader and is eager to learn. They may already to be a team leader, 2IC, or a senior member of the team. Just like Robin in the *Batman* series, they're enthusiastic and want to grow their skills and gain **EXPERIENCE** from the leaders around them. They need more time in their role, watching and learning from others. They're gaining more responsibility in the team and stepping up when asked. They're not the expert yet and still have a lot to learn, but they are motivated to do the work. The sidekick needs to **DEVELOP** their knowledge, skills, and expertise.

The superhero

The superhero has gained expert knowledge and experience in their field. They're well-respected and highly productive. People know who they are in the organisation, and they love to fly in and save the day. They add value by knowing the right answers. People rely on them. The challenge for the superhero is to gain a broader perspective than just their own area of expertise and to develop real **CONFIDENCE** from within, rather than from the superhero status. They need to discover who they are without the cape and gain greater **SELF-AWARENESS** to tap into their true, authentic self.

The coach

The coach focusses on creating collaboration in the team. It's no longer about themselves, but about their people. The coach gives up the desire to rescue and be the expert. They have the confidence to let go of being right and allow others to think for themselves and learn from their mistakes. The coach values each team members' unique contribution and ensures that everyone plays to their strengths. They give and receive feedback freely. The coach must now build **TRUST** in their leadership capacity to take their team's performance to the next level – trust in themselves and trust in their team members. It's time for the coach to **LEVERAGE** their existing influence in the organisation.

The super coach

The super coach has a strong leadership brand and sense of purpose. They know who they are, their values and their legacy, and they are authentic and confident. They inspire and connect people throughout the organisation. They are future focussed and create opportunities for their people to grow and learn. The obstacle for the super coach is to continue to **BALANCE** the needs of their people, organisation and clients, while at the same time taking care of themselves so they can continue to perform at this highest level of leadership. This can be tough and takes ongoing commitment. The super coach must ask themselves, "What's next?", and continually **EXPAND** and broaden their impact and inspiration.

THE 3 STEPS TO BECOMING A SUPER COACH

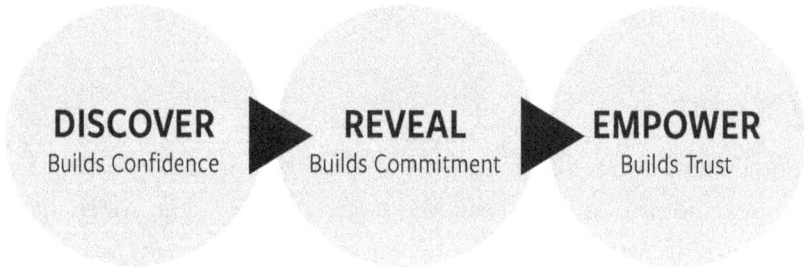

DISCOVER
Builds Confidence

REVEAL
Builds Commitment

EMPOWER
Builds Trust

Step 1: Discover

DISCOVER who you really are as a leader to build CONFIDENCE

Great leadership starts with you. You must first find out who you really are without the superhero cape. You don't need a cape with a personal logo on it to be a leader. You just need to put in the time to discover your values and purpose, and what you stand for.

Genuine and lasting confidence is based on a firm foundation of who you are. It all starts with strong roots. This means developing a solid sense of self. Getting to know yourself and finding your true identity as a leader can be confronting work, but the rewards are boundless.

Discovering yourself requires you to take off the cape and peel back your layers to uncover what's underneath.

Step 2: Reveal

REVEAL your true self to build COMMITMENT

Once you've discovered who you are as a leader, the next step is to show yourself to the world. When you have strong, unwavering confidence, you're able to be vulnerable and let people in. You can share who you are with your team and stop hiding behind a mask.

Revealing yourself to your people is the only way to build lasting commitment. Without people knowing who you are, you might get compliance in the short term: they'll do what you ask of them, but you'll never get heartfelt commitment – the kind of commitment that makes people go above and beyond for you and your clients.

It takes courage as a leader to share yourself and be really seen, but your people will reward you with their loyalty.

Step 3: Empower

EMPOWER your people to build TRUST

The final step to becoming a super coach is to stop rescuing your people and instead empower them to take responsibility and ownership.

Empowering your people allows them to learn and grow. It builds trust in the team and increases creativity and innovation.

It's all about collaboration rather than competition. You have to let go of your power and hand it over to your people. Share the load.

You're not the only one with superpowers. Every one of your team members has their own magic and talent to contribute. Recognise their contribution and make them feel valued and trusted.

Your job as a leader is to help your people succeed. Their performance is your performance.

Part 1

DISCOVER

A superhero derives confidence from external sources.

A supercoach derives confidence from within.

DISCOVER WHO YOU ARE AS A LEADER TO BUILD CONFIDENCE

Your people want a leader with confidence. They want someone they can believe in. Your people will ultimately follow you, not because of the cape you wear but because of who you are.

As a leader, if your self-worth and value are wrapped up in being the superhero, you'll never develop genuine confidence. You'll always need the cape to show everyone you're the boss and the one they should listen to. It's like having a security blanket wrapped around your shoulders.

Superheroes gain their confidence from their appearance, super-powers, costume, possessions (like the Batmobile) or maybe even their superhero gang (like the Avengers).

But what would happen if these external things were taken away? What if they no longer had their costume and superpowers? Would the superhero still have the same confidence? Would they be able to lead? Or would they feel lost and worthless?

Don't be that superhero leader. Instead, gain your confidence and self-worth from who you are on the inside.

In leadership, if you don't put in the time and energy to get to know yourself, you'll always rely on your superhero status. You'll base your self-worth on what others think of you. Your identity will come from the expectations and views of others, not from who you truly are. You'll be cautious and constantly unsure of yourself (although, to the outside world, you might seem like you have it all together).

HOW DO YOU LIKE YOUR EGGS?

Recently, I was having coffee with some colleagues, talking business. It got to 10.30am and I said, "Look, I'm going to have to order something to eat. I'm starving. I'll just order some eggs." In response, one of my colleagues asked, "How do you like your eggs, Midja?" and the others started to laugh. The reference went straight over my head. I mean, what was so funny? Then she said, "You know, Julia Roberts in the *Runaway Bride* movie."

I thought about the reference for a moment and remembered the 1999 romantic comedy starring Julia Roberts and Richard Gere. In the movie, Roberts plays Maggie, a woman who keeps getting engaged, then running out on her fiancés just before the wedding. Gere plays a journalist writing a story on the "runaway bride". He interviews her ex-fiancés, and at the end of each conversation, he asks, "By the way, how does Maggie like her eggs?" Each fiancé gives a different response – scrambled, fried, omelette, poached. You see, Maggie would eat her eggs the same way her fiancé at the time did. Gere's character confronts Maggie about her wedding disasters. The conversation gets quite heated and he blurts, "You're so lost, you don't even know what type of eggs you like!" Ouch.

As a leader, do you know how you like your eggs?

Leadership development starts with self-development and knowing who you are.

Lasting confidence is based on a firm foundation of who you are. It's like a majestic tree that stands tall, unwavering. Its strength comes from a strong root system.

As a leader, you need to develop a solid sense of self. Getting to know yourself and finding your identity as a leader can be confronting, but the rewards are boundless. To truly know yourself, you need to hold a mirror and take a long, hard look at yourself. Sometimes, just the thought of holding that mirror can be scary! Sometimes, you might not want to look in the mirror. You might not like what you see, but it's necessary if you want to gain a deeper level of self-awareness.

If you don't put in the time and energy to get to know yourself, your tree won't develop deep roots. Your confidence will waver, and you'll be constantly unsure of yourself and your direction. You'll be like a tree that sways in the breeze from lack of strength. One minute you stand for this and the next you stand for something else. One day you like your eggs poached, and the next day you want an omelette.

You're unpredictable, and it makes it difficult for your people to follow you. They're not sure who you are and what direction you're heading. And for you as a leader, this swaying in the breeze is exhausting. It's likely that one of your strongest motivations is to be liked as a leader rather than trusted and respected.

Steve Jobs, co-founder of Apple, once said, "If you want to make everyone happy, don't be a leader, sell ice cream." When you're a leader, you're often forced to make the tough decisions for the firm and, ultimately, someone will always be unhappy. In these times, you must be seen as a confident leader. You may also be liked – in fact, I think it's a good start to be likeable as a leader – but it's important to be liked for who you truly are, not who you think your people want you to be.

Finding your identity as a leader requires you to peel back your layers to discover what's underneath. It's about discovering your values, beliefs, purpose, legacy and talents. All these things make you unique. They make you who you are, and great leaders know who they are and dare to be themselves every day. This is what makes them CONFIDENT.

In my first book, *Unshakeable Confidence – How to be Your Most Authentic and Courageous Self*, I discuss what it takes to become an unshakeable leader – a leader who is strong, determined and impactful.

When you're unshakeable, you have a deep understanding of who you are as a leader and how you add the most value to your organisation. You lead with authenticity and congruence. You're comfortable in your skin. You have the confidence to set higher goals for yourself and your team, and you're ready and willing to accept greater responsibilities. You have a determined and tenacious resolution to achieve your goals and make the difference you were meant to make. You stretch yourself and others. You have the courage to take risks and step outside your comfort zone, knowing this is the space of personal growth and development. By doing so, you encourage others to do the same.

Confidence is the key.

"I am not afraid. I was born to do this."

– JOAN OF ARC

In this section, let's reveal the real you to your team.

Let's get you to:

- Create space
- Follow your inner compass
- Relinquish others' expectations
- Experiment
- Stop the comparisons
- Seek feedback
- Uncover your values
- Understand your past story
- Define your legacy
- Find your magic

CREATE SPACE

As a leader, you're busy. It's difficult to find the time to shut out the rest of the world, switch off from the pressures of your job and the needs of your team, and just be. Add to this the busyness of your personal life – housework, friends, errands, children, partner, pets – and it's no wonder having the time to think and discover more about yourself can seem like a pipedream.

But you need to find that time. You need to sit with yourself and discover who you are without the cape. Make it a priority.

Leaders can spend so much time "doing" that they stop "being". The key to gaining confidence as a leader is to know who you are. You need to create thinking space without the noise and distractions to consider how you want to lead and what you want to focus on in your role.

Sometimes, you need to go on autopilot to really give yourself time to think. Neuroscience tells us that when we go on autopilot, our brains get to work. This is the time when our brains start forming new connections.

For me, ideas and insights about myself, my work and my life typically come to me at three times of the day. The first is in the shower. Many mornings, my kids have witnessed me race out of the bathroom to write on the flipchart in the study when something has come to me while washing my hair. The second is when I'm driving. If you check my phone, you'll find lots of one-minute videos of me in the car, capturing an idea. The final time of day is when I'm walking, looking out at the water and keeping a steady pace.

Author and speaker Manoush Zomorodi talks about the brilliance that comes from boredom.

"It might feel weird and uncomfortable at first, but boredom truly can lead to brilliance."

- MANOUSH ZOMORODI

As a kid, I remember continually whining to my mum and dad, "I'm bored. There's nothing to do." Now, as a mum with three kids, it's rare for me to utter those words. Think about your own day…

Early for a meeting? Check your emails. Waiting for a coffee? Scroll through Instagram.

Stuck in traffic? Listen to a podcast.

You can continually keep busy. You can be distracted and multi-task. Technology is a great boredom buster, but at what cost? Your creativity and thinking time.

The noise and busyness of each day get in the way of you learning more about yourself.

The hectic pace of life takes over, and you fall into bed each night exhausted, only to wake the next morning to start the daily grind all over again – another busy day. One week turns into a month and before you know it, another year is done and dusted. You may want to spend time alone, but feel it's impossible to get that time. I've known leaders to hide in coffee shops or unoccupied offices, or even work from home for a morning to grab some quiet thinking space. There can be so many demands on your time and energy.

You can be so busy that it's easy to get distracted by other people's priorities and expectations of you. This leaves little time to focus on your personal development. Sometimes, that might be the way you like it. You can focus on everyone else but yourself, and you get to avoid asking yourself the tough questions, the questions that will challenge your thinking. However, it's your answers to these questions that will provide you with valuable insight into how you can improve in your leadership role, make it your own and move towards your goals. There may be times when your answers surprise you, and you think, "Where did that come from?" A real "aha" moment.

Thoughtful answers help you see situations differently. Your answers could change your attitude and the way you respond to a situation in the future. They could change the way you see yourself. For example, if something went wrong in your day, or perhaps you made a bad decision at work, a simple question such as, "What did I learn from today's decision?", turns a negative situation into a positive one.

Asking questions helps you view every situation as an opportunity to learn more about yourself. It's easier to identify areas that need growth and development. Questions also allow you to examine the meaning of a situation and your response to it so that you can learn more about your beliefs and behaviours.

The intention of self-reflection is not to be over-critical. It's not about judging yourself, blaming others or playing the victim. It's important to be insightful yet playful with your answers. Keep them light. Instead of wasting time navel-gazing and dwelling on the past, acknowledge it and use it to move forward.

Author and life coach Tony Robbins refers to these types of questions as power questions. Robbins says, "Successful people ask better questions, and as a result, they get better answers." So, it's time to think about what questions you could ask yourself to get better answers – and better results. Super coaches are skilled at asking the right questions at the right time – not just of others, but most importantly, of themselves.

"Quality questions create a quality life."

– TONY ROBBINS

American author and business coach Marshall Goldsmith believes asking questions – or "triggers", as he calls them – is key to personal growth, awareness and the ability to lead effectively. Goldsmith has a friend ring him each night to ask him a series of questions, such as: "Did you do your best today to set clear goals, preserve your client relationships or be grateful for what you have?" Goldsmith has done this for years and revises the questions depending on his priorities. He rates his efforts on a scale of one to 10 and ensures he's honest with himself. He calls these questions triggers because they are cues that move you forward in life, in the direction of beneficial change, particularly in a leadership role.

Asking yourself, "What did I learn today to be a better leader tomorrow?", will set you up for success. You will always be looking for ways to improve, learn and develop your attitude and skills. This behaviour, in turn, influences your people, and you will create a culture of continuous self-improvement and a workplace of lifelong learners.

By making self-reflection a habit and asking yourself the right questions, you get clarity on what makes you happy, what brings you joy and what you could do differently in your leadership role. It also helps you detect your purpose, your legacy and what connects you with your values.

You could set yourself reflection questions for the day, the week and the end of the year. It's important to create a ritual that works for you and ask questions that align with your priorities and direction. Your questions should be framed positively and have a useful outcome. For example, asking, "Why don't I have the confidence to speak up at a meeting?" can be reframed as, "What can I do at the next meeting to be more confident to speak up?"

Sometimes, your answers will come straight away; other times, they may take a little longer. You might find it useful to use the same set of questions for a period to gain clarity and a deeper understanding of a behaviour or attitude. Record your questions and answers on paper or digitally. It's useful to look back at what you wrote a year ago to remember where you have been and how far you have come.

Creating pockets of thinking time just for you and asking yourself the right questions will give you deep and valuable insight into who you are as a leader. It will refocus your mind on the positive and provide you with the opportunity to grow and develop. When you create the space to understand yourself and your motivations, it takes away the power of the many distractions in your fast-paced life and directs your focus to what you truly want.

Questions to ask yourself:

- What did I learn today?
- What did I give to others today?
- What am I making excuses for not doing?
- What do I enjoy doing most in my leadership role?
- What can I accept that I can't change?
- Who makes me feel happy at work?
- What was the most important thing I did today?
- What am I most proud of?
- Am I achieving the goals I've set for myself?
- What things do I value most?
- What am I committed to right now?
- When did I last push the boundaries of my comfort zone?

FOLLOW YOUR
INNER COMPASS

H opefully, most of the time, your internal compass faces true north. You feel on track. You're deeply connected with your work and the people in your life. You feel like you're making the right decisions, and you can go about your day ticking things off your to-do list, thinking with your head, making rational decisions.

A little while ago, when I arrived home from school, my eldest son, Tom, greeted me at the door holding a shoebox with holes poked in the lid. I thought to myself, "OK, what do we have here?" I opened the box, and sitting very comfortably inside was the cutest baby bird.

Tom had been walking in the nearby park when he saw the baby bird on the ground being attacked by two other birds. He picked it up and placed it in a nearby tree and came home.

He wasn't home for long, though, before he had this feeling he just couldn't ignore. He said he knew he had to go back to check on the bird. When he returned to the park, the bird was once again on the ground under attack. Tom quickly picked it up and brought the little bird home to safety.

Later that night, Tom and I talked about that feeling inside of him. I explained that his feeling was his internal compass. It represented who he was at his deepest level, his values and beliefs.

Just like Tom, you have an internal compass. There will be times when you feel your internal compass no longer faces true north. You feel out of whack, like something's not right. It's like your compass has got too close to another magnet and starts to spin uncontrollably. That's the time to slow down, stop thinking and start feeling instead.

No one knows you better than you. As a leader trying to discover more about yourself, take the time to listen inwards.

I don't know about you, but my intuition hardly ever lets me down when I take the time to listen to it. This happens even more so as I get older.

Intuition in the corporate setting can suffer from a credibility problem. As a leader, you want to base your conclusions on facts, data and analysis. You want to take a rational approach to your leadership style and listen to the advice of others. This is absolutely a great thing to do (and we'll talk more about receiving feedback soon), but don't discount what your intuition tells you about yourself and how to lead your team.

Remember that your intuition has developed over time. It's shaped by your history, past experiences, knowledge and relationships. It's the result of the patterns your brain has developed. Your intuition is about the connections you've made and your past learnings. It works away behind the scenes, and it needs to be listened to.

A friend recently observed that when I connect with my feelings – my intuition, my true north – I place a hand on my stomach. I wasn't even aware I did this. I put my hand there and consider what it feels like inside.

- Is this the right decision to make?
- Does it feel light or heavy?
- Does it feel warm or cold?

Sometimes, a decision is rationally the right one. It's right "on paper", but emotionally, you know it's not for you.

You know the truth by the way it feels.

So, why do we sometimes ignore this spinning compass inside us?

It might be due to others' expectations or influence. Maybe you feel the pressure to conform. You want to fit in. It might be that you just don't give yourself enough time or space to think deeply about the issue.

And the result? You feel discontented and disappointed. You know you haven't done the right thing.

When you slow down and take the time to recalibrate your compass to true north, you'll:

- Understand yourself more deeply and stay on purpose
- Align yourself with the right people and the right organisation, doing the right work
- Build genuine connections with others

- Make values-based decisions that feel right
- Cope with the most challenging circumstances life presents to you

When you feel something strongly inside of you, stop and lean into it. Act on it. It's that indescribable essence of you that makes you unique. It's the real you.

As a leader, learn to trust your gut. Use it to ask more questions of yourself and dig a little deeper. The most effective leaders listen to their inner wisdom to discover a leadership style that's authentic for them.

"Have the courage to follow your heart and intuition. They somehow know what you truly want to become."

– STEVE JOBS

RELINQUISH OTHERS' EXPECTATIONS

W hen I practised law, people always reacted in a similar way when I told them what I did for work. No matter if it was at a barbecue, dinner or networking event, this is how the conversation would usually go:

Them: So, what do you do for work?

Me: Well, I'm a lawyer, a partner of a national law firm.

Them: Good one. So, what do you really do? (Chuckling)

Me: Seriously, I'm a lawyer.

Them: Wow, you don't look or act like one.

This is the conversation I would have over and over with people, and it would always leave me thinking: as a lawyer, how do they expect me to look and behave? And how come I'm not living up to those expectations? Do they mean it in a good way or a bad way? To tell you the truth, I wasn't sure.

You see, people will have expectations of you in your role. There are certain expectations of you as a leader: what you're supposed to believe in, supposed to say, expected to do, and meant to look like. If you take all those expectations on board and try to live up to them, you will soon start to feel their weight upon you.

Expectations can cage you in. You feel like you can't move, can't breathe. You feel heavy and trapped, like you can't be yourself in your role. You can't lead in a way that feels authentic and easy.

But when you stop focussing on others and turn your focus inward, when you know yourself and can be true to yourself, you free yourself of the cage. You might feel shaky at first, a little uncertain and overwhelmed, because you need to reconnect with yourself. *"Who am I, and what do I want?"* But when you work that out, like a caged tiger that is finally set free, you'll be able to run, and it will feel exhilarating.

However, it can be tough to let go of the expectations of others. You want to be everything to everyone, and you feel like you're constantly judged.

This can be particularly tough when you're stepping into a leadership role in a well-established team. Your team members have told you all about their previous leader, how wonderful they were and how much they're missed. Or maybe you hear the opposite. They couldn't stand their former leader and expect big things from you. They're calling out for a superhero leader to save the day.

In this situation, your default is to want to please them and live up to their expectations. You put on the cape that everyone expects you to wear.

You don't want to disappoint anyone. You want to say yes because you want to be liked. You want to be validated and accepted. But listening to other people's expectations and changing your leadership style because of them means you can start to lose your sense of identity. You second guess yourself, self-doubt creeps in, and your confidence flounders.

People often use the phrase, "I should…": I should do this or I should do that, as a leader. Whenever I hear someone use that phrase, I always ask, "Who thinks you should?" And the answer is "they" do.

So, who are "they"? Sometimes "they" can be your team members or fellow leaders, but often, "they" just refers to a corporate norm you've bought into.

Don't let "them" take control of your leadership role and dictate what you do and don't do. Don't feel guilty for not following their rules. Don't let them change you into someone you're not. Don't let them impact your self-belief and confidence. You'll only be putting on a show, not leading with authenticity. It will be exhausting and, at some point, you'll start to feel resentful.

"The surest way to lose your self-worth is to find it through the eyes of others."

– BECCA LEE

Only one person's expectations matter: yours. The expectations you have placed on yourself by knowing yourself and taking the time to understand your story, values and purpose are the only ones you should listen to. By keeping this front of mind, you can stop being the superhero leader, leave your legacy, and make the difference you're meant to make.

So, push the "shoulds" to one side and ask yourself, "What do I want to achieve in this role? What will make me happy and fulfilled?"

Remember who you were before the world told you who you should be!

EXPERIMENT

To learn and uncover more about yourself, you have to experiment. You need to take some risk.

Discovery doesn't happen when you sit in one place, doing the same thing. Discovery happens when you set sail and explore new things. This is when you find out what you know and what you don't, what you like and what you hate, what turns you on and what leaves you yawning. It results in a deeper connection with who you are.

When I work with a client through a leadership issue, whether it's related to a team member, their leader, a client or process, I always take the approach of "let's keep this open and light, and let's experiment".

It's like those chemistry experiments you did at school. You take a number of elements, put them together in a particular environment (for example, apply heat or freeze them), and see what reaction you get. If you change the quantity of an element or the environment, the outcome will be different.

So, if you want different results, you need to try something different. It's about challenging the current way of thinking and how you see yourself.

Again, you must be prepared to step out of your comfort zone in your leadership role. Put on the white lab coat and protective eyewear. Just like a chemistry experiment, sometimes you need a little more or a little less of an element. Sometimes, you need to be more directive or to stand back and be more curious. Some situations demand you to act quickly; others require a slow and steady approach. In some instances, all it takes is a change in the environment to alter the result.

Give it a go. Fail often and fail fast.

"All life is an experiment. The more experiments you make, the better."

- RALPH WALDO EMERSON

In today's world, you need to be a bold thinker. You must lead innovation and creativity in your team and organisation. By focussing on constant experimentation, you will strengthen your leadership capability and skill set, becoming a confident, courageous, and agile leader – a super coach.

You need to step out of your comfort zone.

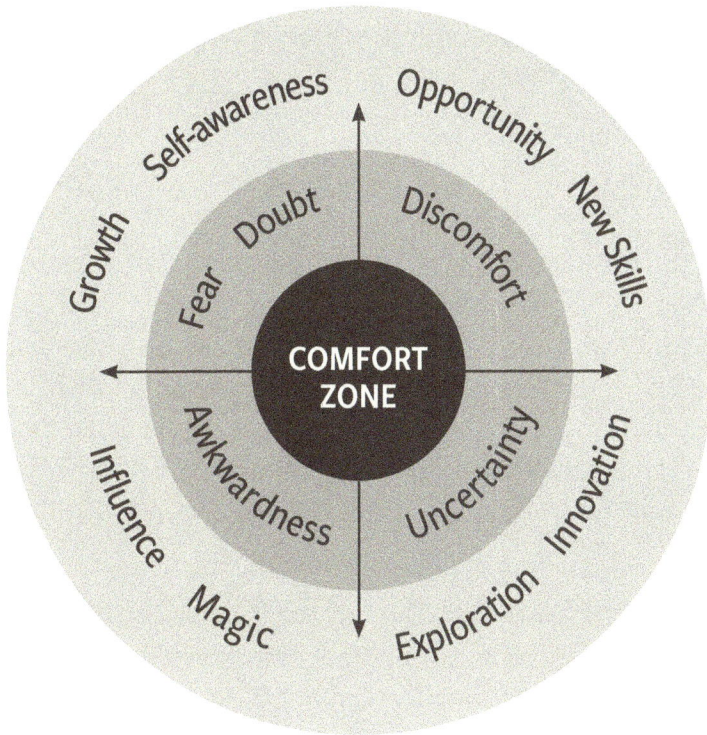

Your comfort zone is a beautiful place. It's where you feel secure and protected. But if you want to play the leadership game and discover who you truly are and what you are capable of, there are times when you need to step out and take a risk. You must get comfortable with being uncomfortable.

There is a part of each of us that loves routine and pattern. In your comfort zone, there is little stress or risk. But there is also little opportunity for you to get to know yourself and what you can achieve. New experiences bring different responses. Sometimes, you need to challenge yourself and see what is revealed.

Neuroscience tells us we need to get out of our comfort zone to rewire our brain. It is possible to train your brain to respond to challenges in new, more effective ways. But to do so, you need to experience new things.

A good friend of mine always asks,

"What else is possible?"

I love this question. Until you try, you don't know. So, try something new. You may surprise yourself. I read once that the role of a leader is climate control – to create a climate of possibilities. In this climate, you and your team members will develop new skills and capabilities to face even greater challenges. Leadership is not about standing still and accepting the status quo. It's about improvement, innovation, exploration and, at times, pushing the boundaries.

Stepping outside your comfort zone can feel awkward and uncomfortable. But outside your comfort zone is a place of great opportunity. If you want to be a great leader and super coach, you must commit to being a lifelong learner.

You must continually work your way through the Four Stages of Learning or, as it's often referred to, the Conscious Competence Ladder. This model (next page) was developed by Noel Burch, an employee with Gordon Training International, in the 1970s. It highlights two factors that affect our thinking as we learn a new skill: consciousness (awareness) and skill level (competence).

According to the Conscious Competence Ladder, we move through the various levels as we build competence in a new skill.

I spent 20 years in the corporate world both as a lawyer and as an in-house facilitator and coach. I was at the highest level on the ladder, **unconsciously competent**. I got to the stage where I didn't have to think about what I was doing; it just came naturally. I could get up in the morning, facilitate a course, run an induction program, coach a colleague, and not have to consciously think about it. I knew who I was, how I added value, and the legacy I wanted to leave in that organisation.

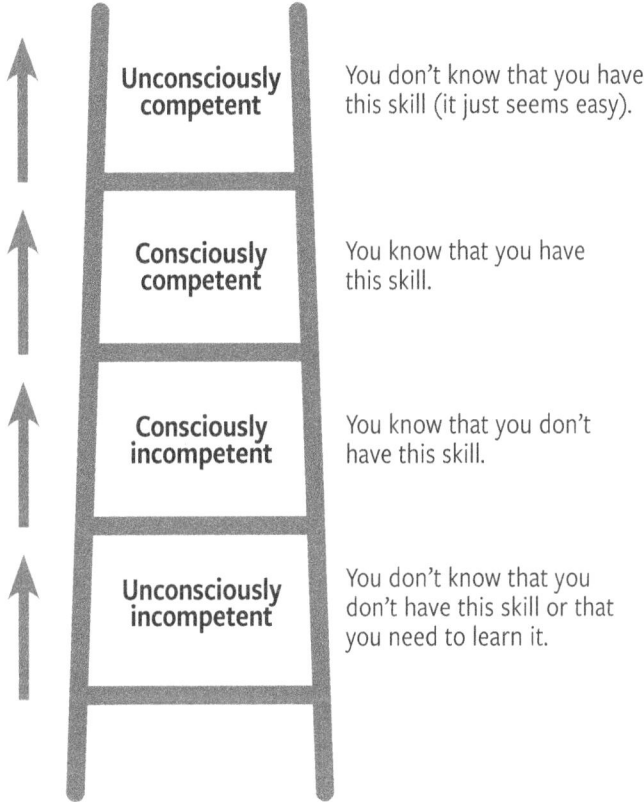

Unconsciously competent	You don't know that you have this skill (it just seems easy).
Consciously competent	You know that you have this skill.
Consciously incompetent	You know that you don't have this skill.
Unconsciously incompetent	You don't know that you don't have this skill or that you need to learn it.

It feels great at the top of the ladder, but stay there too long, and you're well and truly in your comfort zone.

When you take the bold leap out of your comfort zone and into a new leadership position, you step back down the Conscious Competence Ladder to **unconsciously incompetent**. You don't know what you don't know. The result of this is actually very positive (at least, for a while). You feel optimistic, excited and ready to take on the challenge. No fear. You think to yourself, "I can do this!" Your motivation, engagement and confidence levels are high.

But what happens? At some point, the bubble bursts. It bursts sooner for some people than others. You start to learn and gain some experience. You make mistakes; you feel lost. Things take a long time to do. You might start getting negative feedback from your boss, colleagues and clients. You engage a mentor who asks you some tough questions you don't know the answers to. You look around and notice that others are ahead of you in this new game of leadership. They know more than you, and they have a lot more proficiency. You're not sure who you are anymore or how you add value.

I experienced this when I first set up my own leadership practice. I was ready to go, **unconsciously incompetent**. All smiles. Then I realised there was a whole lot more to this game than I was aware of. Marketing, positioning, sales, social media, website development, invoicing, book publication, finance... absolutely overwhelming!

This becomes the pivotal moment, your moment of choice. You feel extremely vulnerable, uncomfortable and out of your depth. Sometimes, you feel plain stupid. You hate feeling this way. What makes it worse is that you've previously been at the top of your game. You've been highly successful, recognised and rewarded. This change can knock your confidence and be downright scary.

If you want to keep moving forward, now is the time for you to push through the stage of **consciously incompetent**. It takes courage to take time out to find yourself again. Sometimes, it feels a whole lot easier to go back to what you know and what you are good at. It can be so tempting.

But if you keep doing the hard work, you will become **consciously competent**, and one day you will reach the top of the ladder again and become **unconsciously competent** in your new role as the super coach. It's going to feel clunky at times, and it's going to take a lot of commitment, but it's worth it. You'll regain that feeling of control and confidence, and you'll be willing to learn more and step even further outside your comfort zone. Always learning, growing and discovering more about who you really are and what you have to give.

STOP THE
COMPARISONS

D o you ever compare yourself to others? How well do you stack up? Do you allow these comparisons to determine your self-worth and confidence?

I know I've been guilty of comparing my life to the lives of my friends, family and colleagues – comparing my success, career, intelligence, leadership abilities, relationships and wealth. As a young lawyer, I remember looking at the other lawyers in the firm and comparing myself to them. *"She's billed more than me this month. He's so much better at negotiating than I am. Clients seem to really connect with her."* What a waste of energy!

Time spent comparing yourself to others is time you could spend discovering who you are. Comparisons are unnecessary, unhelpful and rarely accurate. If you compare yourself to others and base your self-worth on these comparisons, you do yourself an injustice.

There was a time when people looking at my life from the outside would have thought it was perfect. I was married with three kids, living on the Gold Coast, and a partner in a law firm. People thought my life was flawless. But looks can be deceiving. When I told people my marriage was over, I was leaving my law firm and hadn't been in a good place in my life for a long time, they were shocked.

You see, people only show you a small piece of their life. Then you take that piece, interpret it and compare it to your life. It's so easy to do. Of course, now it's easier than ever with social media. We can see what our "friends" are doing every time of the day and night.

It's easy to spend hours of your time consuming other people's lives via their social media feeds. You forget that these posts do not equal real life. A post is just a happy snapshot. It's a tiny part of someone's life that they have selected and filtered. I know I've posted a smiling, loving family photo at dinner, only to be screaming at the kids 10 minutes later. I'm not posting, "Here I am on a Tuesday night doing my third load of washing #whoseideawas3kids", or, "Here I am on a Saturday night home by myself again #midjacantgetadate".

You see, Facebook, LinkedIn and Instagram feeds are people's highlight reels. They consist of the moments people are proud of and want to share. It's the perception they want you to have of their life; not their real life at all.

In leadership, it's critical to your self-belief that you put all this into context and see it for what it is. If you spend your time and energy looking at other people's lives – their accomplishments and achievements – and feel sorry for yourself, you'll have nothing to give to your people. You'll lack the confidence and courage to lead with influence, hiding behind the cape, trying to be someone you're not.

Every leader is distinctive. You bring your own way of thinking, strengths and talents to your leadership role, so stop trying to be like everyone else.

> *I remember when I was mentoring a group of facilitators and gave them feedback on their delivery style. During one of our sessions, one of my mentees said she finally knew what was holding her back. She had been trying to imitate me and how I presented to the group, and it was such hard work for her. She explained that once she stopped comparing herself to me, she found her own style of delivery, and it worked. It came naturally, and she absolutely nailed it.*

Of course, it's natural and, I think, helpful to aspire to be like others around you. It's good to have influential leaders you want to follow, but you need to be mindful of any negative impact. You need to be able to identify when someone is motivating and inspiring you, and when they are negatively impacting your self-esteem.

If someone brings out the best in you and makes you strive to achieve your own leadership goals, keep them in your life. But if someone makes you feel less than good enough, then you need to remove them. Otherwise, they'll continue to drain your energy and stop you from doing your best work.

If they're on social media, stop following them. Unfriend them. If they're in the office, stop giving them your time and energy. It's like anything in life – if it's not bringing you something positive, get rid of it. Do a clean-out.

Stop idolising other leaders and start humanising them. There is always more than meets the eye to every situation and person.

Everyone is unique, and we all go through different stages in our lives and careers: the ups and downs, swings and roundabouts.

We all continue to learn and grow. We all have our strengths and weaknesses as leaders. Once you stop the comparisons, you can be genuinely happy for others and their achievements, knowing you have your unique strengths. Even if things may not be going so well for you, your time will come. As one of my friends says, "Tide comes in, and tide goes out."

When you stop comparing yourself to others, you can focus on discovering yourself: who are really are and how you can gain influence as a leader. It's an opportunity for you to be happy in your skin, knowing you have a unique contribution to make and your own way of inspiring others in your team.

"Comparison is the thief of joy."

– THEODORE ROOSEVELT

SEEK FEEDBACK

We've discussed the importance of deepening your self-awareness and self-perception to find your identity as a leader – who you are without the cape. But what's also important is the perception of others – your colleagues, clients, and the people you lead.

Don't care what others think of you? Maybe you should (just a little).

What do other people hear, see, and, most importantly, feel when they are around you? What do others genuinely think of you?

I have the wonderful opportunity to meet some amazing people in various leadership positions. It always intrigues me to hear them explain how they feel on the inside. To listen to them talk about their self-perception, who they are, their values and beliefs, and what they do for their clients. As they talk, it's hard for me not to compare their self-perception to my perception of them from the outside.

It's like the iceberg analogy. You know what's going on under the water (your internal feelings), but others have a much better understanding of what's going on above the water (your external presentation). They have a better view.

I'm not backwards when it comes to sharing with people what I consider to be their "magic". I believe everyone should understand their strengths and talents and have the opportunity to dial them up. However, for most of us, our cognitive blind spot (that part of ourselves we fail to see due to our biases) gets in the way of us seeing all that we are.[5] We can't get a realistic view of what's on top of the water.

American psychologist Carl Rogers said that genuine self-awareness could be honed if we took the time to join our self-awareness (who we think we are) with the perception of what others see in us.[6] In other words, we need to join what's above the water with what's below. The idea is that to understand yourself fully, you need the perspective of others. This perspective gives you the belief and mindset to become your ideal self, the very best version of you – that authentic, genuine, confident, super coach leader!

So, how do you do this? You need to open your heart and mind to receiving feedback. You need the confidence to accept others' gift of insight – good and bad.

5   Vazire, S. and Carlson, E. "Others Sometimes Know Us Better Than We Know Ourselves", *Current Directions in Psychological Science*, 15 April, 2011. https://journals.sagepub.com/doi/abs/10.1177/0963721411402478
6   Rogers, C. (1959). "A theory of therapy, personality and interpersonal relationships as developed in the client-centered framework". In (ed.) S. Koch, *Psychology: A Study of a Science. Vol. 3: Formulations of the person and the social context.* New York: McGraw Hill.

Often when I give positive feedback to others, they get embarrassed, avoid eye contact, lean back, and mumble something like, "I'm not sure about that," or, "Do you really think so?"

When someone compliments us, we usually reject it in one of three ways. Response number one is the put down: "What do you mean the presentation went well? I completely fumbled over the start." Response number two is the deflection: "No, I thought Tom's presentation last week was much more succinct." Response number three highlights our inner sceptic: "Really? You think so? I'm not so sure."

Do any of these responses sound familiar? I know I've said them myself. It's time to stop! Think of positive feedback as extra nourishment for your leadership confidence. Accept a compliment with grace and allow it to reaffirm your strengths and add to your leadership brand.

On the flip side, when I give negative feedback, the recipient often gets defensive. I know I can do the same.

I remember a training co-ordinator coming up to me a few years ago to give me feedback on some assessments I had marked. She felt that some of my marking was inconsistent. Before she could even finish giving me the feedback, I made excuses and blamed others. She then backed away and said sorry. She apologised for trying to give me honest feedback – feedback I needed about my lack of attention to detail. A few hours later, what I had just done kicked in and I apologised to her.

Sometimes, we don't want to hear feedback. It's tough; it's personal. But if we ever want people to be honest with us again, we've got to suck it up and listen, really listen, with the intent to understand.

To get honest feedback that contributes to your leadership identity, you need to do the following:

- **Ask for feedback.** Be proactive. Don't sit in your office, waiting for someone to knock on your door. The old saying that "no news is good news" doesn't apply to the assessment of your leadership skills. You must make asking for feedback a habit. Do it every week.

- **Be specific when you ask.** Asking someone how they think you're going in your role or slipping in the question, "So, do you have any feedback for me?", at the end of a conversation or meeting is ineffective. You won't get anything worthwhile from that. It's too safe. Instead, ask for something specific. For example, "In our weekly meetings, I've been conscious that I do most of the talking. I'm keen for these meetings to be collaborative, to get everyone's opinions. Can I get your feedback after the meeting this week about how I went with it, and if you felt everyone had the chance to contribute? Thanks." You'll find people will be willing to give you more honest, helpful feedback with this approach.

- **Really listen to feedback.** If it's negative feedback, don't interrupt it with your BEDtime story of blame, excuses and denials (see below).

- **Acknowledge feedback and take action.** Thank the person for their feedback, positive or negative. Make them feel valued for taking the time to give you their opinion. Ask for further clarification if you need to gain a deeper understanding, then consider whether you need to take any action. Think of it as an opportunity to learn more about yourself and grow as a leader.

Often when we make a mistake or receive negative feedback, we react immediately and bring out our BEDtime stories:

- **Blame.** The greatest game on earth is the blame game. It was the CEO, the board, one of your team members, the admin staff, the client, etc. It was anyone's and anything's fault but your own. When things go wrong, you can panic and start to throw people under the bus to take attention away from your culpability.

- **Excuses.** You can come up with a million and one excuses why something hasn't gone to plan. Some of these reasons can be valid. Bad stuff happens to good people. Often, as a leader, we use a lack of resources as an excuse: "I didn't have enough people/time/money to make it happen." But is this taking ownership of your actions and leadership role?

- **Denial.** You can hide the mistake and pretend it didn't happen. You can sweep it under the carpet and move on – that is until someone else finds out about it!

BEDtime stories can be a default response when you feel under threat and out of control. They're an almost instinctive reaction to protect yourself. But they have a significant impact on your relationship with your people.

If someone is willing to give you feedback, good or bad, take the time to truly listen to what they have to say. You could discover something new about yourself; something that's been sitting beneath the surface.

And, as a leader, don't just wait for feedback – be proactive and ask for it. It's part of the gig and a habit you must practise regularly. The wonderful by-product of asking for feedback is that you develop relationships based on honesty and trust, as well as discover more about yourself.

UNCOVER YOUR VALUES

O ne of the keys to discovering yourself and defining who you are as a leader is knowing your top personal values. Your values form your leadership foundation and announce to your people what is truly important to you.

Values are your preferences and priorities in life. They provide you with meaning and motivation. We all have them, whether we're aware of them or not. Your values help you make sense of your world and interpret your life experiences. They influence the way you lead and the decisions you make. Your values are personal to you and, in this regard, are different from morals and ethics.

Morals are principles of what is right and wrong. They are judgments, whereas values are neither right nor wrong. They simply are. Sometimes, your values can seem so "right" to you that you believe everyone prioritises them the way you do. But they are only your personal values and are no better or worse than anyone else's.

> *I remember leading a team of people and being so frustrated by one of the administration clerks, who didn't share my passion for learning and study. I thought she could be an outstanding lawyer and that she should start her university studies, but she just wasn't interested. She wasn't interested because this course of action didn't align with her values. I had projected my values onto her life situation.*

Ethics are an accepted set of standards or behaviours, usually developed by a professional society within a particular profession. Ethics govern and constrain your behaviour. Values also impact your behaviour, but two people can share the same value and be motivated to behave differently. For example, think about the value of family and belonging. This is usually a high-priority value for a new mum, and it is also a high-priority value for a member of the Mafia. It's safe to assume the behaviours associated with this value would vary considerably between these two people.

In the words of Paul Chippendale, founder of Minessence International: "It doesn't matter what values you have, what matters is how you live them." As you can see from the above example, the same value can be lived in very different ways.

Your values are personal and will change over time. They will likely shift as you progress throughout your career and gain more experience and knowledge.

SO, WHERE DO YOUR VALUES COME FROM?

Age/Gender	Experiences	Peers
Education	Upbringing	Friends
Religion	Culture	Environment
IQ	Family	Work

Each of us is driven by our values. They guide our decision making and behaviour, whether we like it or not. Your power comes from being able to move your values from your unconscious to your conscious mind. In other words, when you know what your values are, you have greater control over your decisions and direction, which is essential for any leader. If your values are stuck in your unconscious, it's difficult to know why you react the way you do. In the words of Swiss psychiatrist Carl Jung, "Until you make the unconscious conscious, it will direct your life and you will call it fate." Without knowing your values, you struggle to understand your biases and view of the world.

You might ask yourself:

- Why do I struggle to be motivated doing this type of work?
- Why am I procrastinating?
- Why am I reacting so negatively?
- Why does this new work policy push my buttons?

If you don't consciously connect with your values, you can't put into words your why, your purpose or how you feel. And when you can't do that, you fail to make your feelings known to others. Values make communication and understanding as a leader so much easier.

Your values filter the way you see the world. For example, let's say an opportunity to work interstate is presented to two people. If one of them has a high value of family and belonging, they may feel anxious because it means they will be away from their partner or children. However, if the other person has a high value of financial security and the work means a wage increase, they might jump at the chance.

If you've ever had a goal you couldn't achieve, or if you've lacked the motivation to put in the hard yards, chances are the goal was not connected to one of your high-priority personal values. It might have been something you thought you "should" do, but because it wasn't linked to your values, there was no real drive to achieve it. It held no significant meaning for you. If you want to succeed with your goal setting, make sure you link your goals to one of your top values.

Your values also dictate what excites you and what bores you to tears. When I'm in a meeting or at a friend's barbecue, I like to observe people's reactions to the conversation. As soon as someone's eyes light up or I see them get on the defensive, I know the conversation has hit one of their top values – or a nerve! You can't help but react when your values are impacted.

Another advantage of knowing your values is that it's easier to seek work projects and opportunities that connect with you. If you can align your values and your work, bingo! You create flow. This is when work doesn't feel like work – you're on point, you're in the zone, you can work for hours on end and you don't know where the time has gone. Have you ever felt this way? If you have, it means your work has connected with your values.

Super coaches understand their values and behave in a way that is consistent with them every single day. As a leader, your values are the key to influencing and understanding your people. Knowing your values means you can be authentic and build trust with others. Your people know who you are and what makes you tick. They understand you. They may not always agree with you, but they understand why you've made a particular decision.

So, take the time to discover your values as a leader. The principal values profiling tool I use is the Minessence Values Framework.[7] It consists of 128 values and their descriptors, which are maintained and continually developed by an international group of experts. You can complete an online questionnaire that processes your responses to create your personalised values map, identifying which of the 128 possible values are a priority for you.

You can also gain a more informal view of your values by asking yourself questions associated with your preferences and priorities, like:

- Think of a time when you felt completely at ease and fulfilled. What was it about this situation that made you feel like this?
- Think of a time when someone or something irritated you and pushed your buttons. What made you feel this way?
- Think of those in your past or present who you consider your heroes. What qualities do they have that prompted you to put them on your list?
- If you had to move to another planet and could only take five things with you, what would they be? Why? What do those five things represent to you?

Your values are integral to who you are. As a leader, you must gain a clear understanding of your top values, what they are and what they mean to you. Then share those values with your team and

---

7   https://www.mvf-knowledge-base.com/p/mvf.html

keep them front of mind in your everyday decision making. When your values and actions are in alignment, your character as a leader strengthens, and your confidence grows.

"Values are like fingerprints. Nobody's are the same, but you leave 'em all over everything you do."

– ELVIS PRESLEY

UNDERSTAND
YOUR PAST STORY

Behind every superhero is an origin story, telling how they gained their powers and why they decided to fight crime. It's a story not often shared with those they protect, but one they hold deep inside. Their backstory remains a mystery, along with their true identity. The superhero's story is typically locked away in their unconscious mind, with only glimpses shown to them as flashbacks.

As a super coach, it's time to interpret and share your past story to discover who you are as a leader. Your story is unique. It's yours, full of learning and wisdom. Whether you're aware of it or not, you attribute meaning to all the important events in your life, and that meaning shapes you as a leader, becomes part of who you are. It's time to unlock your leadership story.

Of course, the same event or circumstance can mean different things to different people. The great thing is that you get to connect the dots in your story the way *you* want. You don't have to worry about anyone else's interpretation, just your own. For example, people can work in the same organisation, even in the same team, and take away something different. The same goes for siblings in a family – they have experienced the same upbringing and family events, but may interpret those events differently and take a different meaning from them.

Your origin story gives you valuable insight into your why, your beliefs, values and behaviours. Your story, up until this point, has shaped who you are as a leader. The important events of your life contribute to your leadership style. They have also created your leadership message to the world.

You've gained a range of skills and knowledge from your experiences and the obstacles you've overcome. You've learned from the good times and bad. It's important to take the time to look at the events, encounters and circumstances that have brought you to where you are today. There is value in examining your life story. As a leader, it can help you elevate your thinking and understand what you bring to the leadership table, what makes you unique.

While examining your story, look for patterns. Sometimes, we find ourselves learning the same lessons over and over. You may repeat the same behaviours, even though they may not work for you. You may have the same kind of relationships. Without examining your story, you fail to see that the behaviours that worked for you in the past may not work for you now. Why is that? What's changed? No doubt a lot has changed, but you haven't adjusted your behaviour accordingly.

As you get to know your story, examine the times of transition in your life. When did they occur and why? How did you deal with them? What did the "before and after" look like?

Look for gaps in your life story. Has something been missing, something you have needed? What do you plan to do about it? Start closing the gap between what has happened in your story and where you want the story to end.

Of course, you can't change your past story. The past is the past. But you can gain great insight from it. You don't want to spend too much time dwelling on it or losing yourself in thoughts of what might have been. *"If only I had done that…"* Knowing your story is not about navel-gazing or paralysis by analysis; instead, it's about keeping the process light, acknowledging your past events, understanding them, and learning what you can to gain a better understanding of yourself in your role as a super coach. Use this knowledge to move forward and focus on the future. There may be times when focussing on a past event in great detail can be beneficial, and that's part of the counselling process. If this is the case, I recommend you seek counsel from a professional.

Your past can weigh heavily on you if you don't acknowledge and accept it. It can consume your thoughts and sap your energy. Don't let the past define you, but instead understand it so you can make informed choices.

"Sometimes you just have to make peace with your past in order to keep your future from becoming a constant battle."

– SUSAN GALE

Without understanding your story, you'll struggle to gain that deeper understanding of who you are and how you got here. You'll continue to feel frustrated and confused about why you react the way you do in certain situations. You question yourself:

- "Where did that response come from?"
- "Why do I feel like this?"
- "Why did I say that?"
- "Why does this keep happening to me?"

Your story evolves; it keeps being written and re-written. So, too, do your beliefs, values and behaviours. Your story gives your life context. It doesn't give you an excuse to blame, play the victim or whinge, but it does make you say, "Ah, that's why I think this way and that's why it's one of my values." It allows you to be kinder to yourself, make changes in your life, and take deliberate action to form new habits if you want to take a different direction.

So, super coach, think about your story.

What has shaped you? How has your story influenced you as a leader?

Consider your childhood loves, your interests, family, schooling, geography, upbringing, where you have travelled to, your holidays, role models, and work history.

Consider the events that have triggered emotions, either positive or negative. When have you felt joy, excitement, happiness, pride, guilt, loss, fear, resentment? What did these events mean to you at the time? What do they mean to you now? What was the result? What did you learn?

Consider the people who have been your greatest influencers at different times of your life.

- Who has influenced you the most?
- Why were they part of your life at that time?
- What did you learn from them?

As a leader, your story will give you greater appreciation and understanding of yourself. It will point to your passion and purpose, enabling you to lead with the confidence of knowing where you have come from and where you wish to go.

"Loving ourselves through the process of owning our story is the bravest thing we'll ever do."

– BRENÉ BROWN

DEFINE YOUR
LEGACY

S adly, in 2017, I attended the funerals of several people close to me – including my dad's. It was a tough year (we've all had some of those). As I stood in the church, looking around at my family and friends, listening to their stories about my dad during the service and, later, over a few beers, my heart burst with love and pride. My dad's life was a life well spent, and he left an everlasting impact on others. My sister and I often talk about how dad's voice is still in our heads, giving us advice, although now we're in a better position to ignore it if we want to. (Sorry, Dad!)

Later that night after the funeral, when I was alone and tucked in bed, my thoughts turned to my own funeral (a little morbid, I know, but it's the truth). I asked myself, "Would the people present have warm hearts and fond memories of me? What would they say about me and my legacy? How would I be remembered?"

I have a very clear vision of the legacy I want to leave. Do you?

When you think about your work as a leader, how do you want to be remembered? If your funeral is a little morbid to think about, how about your five- or 10-year work anniversary? Who would be there to celebrate with you? What would they say about your leadership?

"One day, your life will flash before your eyes. Make sure it's worth watching."

– GERARD WAY

Consider what would feature on the highlight reel of your career. What moments would be worthy of inclusion?

As a leader, once you're clear on your top personal values, it's time to take those values and use them to connect with your legacy and purpose. This is your why.

Author and marketing guru Simon Sinek says we must all start with our why. Too many of us get caught up in *what* we do, but the first question we must always ask is *why* we do it.

"Working hard for something we don't care about is called stress; working hard for something we love is called passion."

– SIMON SINEK

Why do you get up every morning? Why are you a leader? Focussing on your legacy allows you to jump out of bed each day with energy and purpose. Through your leadership role, you'll create a lasting influence on the people, organisations and causes you are involved in, which will one day add up to something others perceive as your legacy. Now is the time to stop and consider what your legacy will be.

When you define your leadership legacy, you give your role purpose. You can lead with a clear objective and an end goal in mind. You know who you are and what your life is about. Your legacy gives you clarity in your decision making. It helps you decide when to say yes and when to say no – something that can be tough to do in our busy lives. Your legacy makes your leadership choices so much easier. All you need to do is ask yourself, "Does this contribute to who I am and how I want to make a difference?"

The impact you have as a leader can make an enormous difference in the lives of others. Think about how your thoughts and actions impact your people and, in turn, their relationships with their clients, colleagues, and even their partner and children. Our work plays such a huge part of our lives and, as a leader, your impact is significant.

I think all of us could tell a story about a leader we'll never forget, someone who changed our lives for the better, and who has, therefore, touched the lives of so many others. You have the opportunity to be one of those leaders – a leader whose story is shared by others and remembered long after you leave your organisation.

For some people, the impact they make will be public and far-reaching – perhaps on the world stage. For others, like my dad, their impact will be the profound difference they make to the lives of those closest to them: their inner circle, partner, friends, children and colleagues.

The nature of your impact doesn't matter. It's personal and unique to you. What is important is that your legacy connects with your values, priorities and what you believe in.

Defining your legacy is like beginning with the end in mind, which is Habit 2 in Dr Stephen Covey's book, *The 7 Habits of Highly Effective People*. If you can define your purpose and the difference you want to make, you can start making your leadership legacy a reality now by putting into place congruent thoughts, behaviours and actions.

If your legacy is not defined, you risk spending your time and energy on things that don't matter. You can end up second guessing yourself and your decisions, feeling like what you do doesn't make a difference. You waste your position of influence worrying about the what-ifs.

Often, people don't consider their legacy until they face a life-changing event or their mortality. When this happens, some people look back on their lives with satisfaction, content knowing they wouldn't change a thing. Others feel compelled to make changes immediately, if they still have the opportunity. They want to ensure they say and do the things that matter, the things that will leave a lasting impact.

You can't change your past, but you can decide right now what your purpose is and the difference you want to make. You can create the legacy you want in your leadership role. It's about taking the time to define and discover what that legacy is, then committing yourself to the necessary steps to ensure it comes true. What does the "real" you (not the superhero wearing the cape) want to achieve in your role?

"I've come to believe that each of us has a personal calling that's as unique as a fingerprint - and that the best way to succeed is to discover what you love and then find a way to offer it to others in the form of service, working hard, and also allowing the energy of the universe to lead you."

– OPRAH WINFREY

FIND YOUR MAGIC

Unlike the most famous superheroes, you don't need to be exposed to a gamma bomb (the Hulk), bitten by a radioactive spider (Spider-Man) or even come from an alien planet (Superman) to have the power to be a great leader.

Inside of you is your own leadership magic: a set of unique skills and abilities that make you YOU. You don't need superpowers. You already have a special gift to use in your leadership role.

"It is important to remember that we all have magic inside us."

- J.K. ROWLING

Your leadership magic is unique to you. Call it your talent, natural skill, strength, gift, whatever – it doesn't matter what you call it. What matters is that you discover it and use it to its full potential.

Your magic will contribute to your greatest strength as a leader: what you're known for. Your magic will captivate others and build your reputation and leadership brand. It's the gift you have to share with your people.

I've mentored leaders who have tried to fight their natural skill, their magic. One female leader had a real gift for attention to detail. She was a perfectionist by nature. She could pick up an error, conduct a SWOT analysis, and assess a situation for gaps like no one else, but she hated her talent and thought it was boring. She believed anyone could do what she did. But they couldn't. For her, it was innate. Whether you want to argue for nature or nurture or a combination, it doesn't matter. She had a gift. So, my advice to her was to embrace her gift and make it her own.

If you fight your magic, it feels unnatural. Leadership becomes hard. You feel you're wasting your time and not moving forward, but you're also not sure what you're supposed to do. It gnaws at you. You know there is something more you must give, but you don't know what it is. It's your job to find that magic.

Sometimes, your magic will find you. It's easy to recognise and identify. But sometimes, it's hidden deep inside, and only the right circumstances or opportunity will bring it out. Finding your magic may mean trying new things and seeing what feels right, particularly when you're starting in a leadership position. If you think about the leaders in your current organisation or leaders you have worked with in the past, you will discover that they all had their unique magic, something that made them different from everyone else. What's your difference?

- **What do people in your organisation and team come to you for?**

  Is it for your positivity, empathy, decisiveness, humour, attention to detail, determination, bravery or reasoning? Perhaps it's a skill such as writing, speaking or selling. Whatever it is, pay attention to it.

- **What comes naturally to you?**

  I like to call this the "duh" moment. It's that thing you do, say or feel that you think is easy. It's something you think everyone does. But guess what? It's not what everyone does. It's what *you* do. It's so natural to you that you don't even have to think about it. You don't realise it's your magic. You may not place any value on it because it doesn't take much effort. It's time to take notice of this talent and not ignore it.

- **What's the best part of your day?**

  What's that thing you do at work that doesn't feel like work? I hear people say they would continue to do a certain type of work or an aspect of their job even if they didn't get paid for it. What is this for you?

- **What excites you?**

  What gets your adrenaline going? What do you look forward to? There might be some anxiety and fear around it, but it's that mixture of excitement and fear you need to recognise.

So, what's your magic, and how can you use it to become a super coach? In fact, don't just use it – amplify it to become extraordinary.

When I open my eyes each morning, a message stares back at me in a white frame with beautiful gold writing. It says, "You did not wake up today to be mediocre." Each morning, I read that message and say to myself, "No, you did not." And neither did you.

Leaders often ask me, "Should I spend my time focussing on my magic, my strengths, the things I'm already good at? Or should I try to improve my weaknesses, the gaps in my skills?" My answer is to always play to your strengths.

To me, it comes down to this. You can either be ordinary at everything or extraordinary at something. If you focus on your weaknesses, you may become well rounded. People often think that's a great thing. They put their energy and focus on improving their weaknesses to be a jack of all trades. However, you've got to ask yourself, "Do I want to be described as well-rounded or extraordinary?" I know which one I want to be.

If you play to your strengths, you can become extraordinary. The most inspiring leaders are known for something. They know their ace card, and they know how to use it. They play to their strengths because they know that in doing so, they make the biggest difference in the lives of others. To be a great leader, you need to focus on your magic. You need to give it all the energy it deserves. You must amplify it and dial it up. I'm talking high definition!

Of course, you need to be aware of your weaknesses and find ways to contain them, but your time as a leader is best spent doing what you do well. Malcolm Gladwell, in his book *Outliers*, refers to the 10,000-hour rule, based on the research of Herbert Simon and William Chase. According to this rule, it takes 10,000 hours – in other words, a lot of time and practice – to become proficient at a complex task. If it takes that much time and effort to become exceptional at something, don't waste it on things that will make you mediocre or average. Keep the spotlight on your strengths, where you are centre stage and shine.

When you play to your strengths, you take the lead. Why would you step away from centre stage to make room for something you're not good at, something you don't enjoy and doesn't come naturally to you? The spotlight shines brightest when you do your best work, the work you're meant to do, contributing in the most meaningful way possible. This is where you have the most significant impact on your people.

At a young age, I knew I loved to talk. I remember the joy that came from my show-and-tell days at school. It was my favourite time of the week. While my friends dreaded getting up in front of the class, I was nearly wetting my pants with excitement. This love of presenting stayed with me and grew. Over my career, I took every opportunity to present anything at any time to anyone. In addition to managing a law office and servicing my clients, I would facilitate, train and present. I presented at team meetings, firm strategy days, Law Association days, induction courses, anything. Why? Because I wanted to get to that 10,000 hours of facilitating and speaking. I knew it wasn't going to happen by accident. I had to be deliberate about it.

If you don't actively seek opportunities to amplify your strengths, you'll never fully discover what you're capable of. Imagine what's possible if you stopped focussing on your weaknesses and gave your full focus to strengthening your magic, your gift. Think about what you could achieve.

The great news is you have more resources at your fingertips now than ever before to practise and hone your talent: online courses,

TED Talks, public workshops, podcasts, research papers, YouTube clips, the list goes on.

A mentor is another highly valuable option. A mentor is someone you aspire to be in your field of expertise. They've been there, done that, and bought the T-shirt! They are inspiring and extremely knowledgeable. You can learn a lot from your mistakes, but you can learn a lot more from the mistakes of a mentor. My own mentors have been amazing sources of knowledge and motivation. Who do you admire and aspire to be? Reach out to them and ask whether they would be willing to take you under their wing.

Remember, the greatest impact comes from amplifying your talent. As a leader, when you use your strengths to make a difference in the lives of your people, they'll forgive you your weaknesses. In fact, they may not even notice them. So, give your magic your full focus and attention. Give 100%. I say if you're going to do something, do it big!

Don't settle for good enough or mediocre.

Strive to be extraordinary.

Part 2

REVEAL

A superhero hides behind their mask and only gains compliance.

A super coach shows their true self and gains commitment.

REVEAL WHO YOU ARE AS A LEADER TO BUILD COMMITMENT

A superhero goes to great lengths to hide their true identity, often living a double life. They put on their cape and mask to save the day, then return to their "normal" life. No one knows who they really are. They don't allow anyone to get close enough to know the real them.

Superheros are admired and respected for their superhero status, not for who they are. They gain compliance from their people, but not heartfelt, genuine commitment. This type of commitment is built by super coaches, who have the confidence to be vulnerable and let people see the real them.

As a super coach, you share your story and have the courage to tell the truth. There's no hiding behind a mask. You know you don't have to be perfect to be a strong leader; you can admit to your mistakes and ask for help.

You will never feel as strong as you do once you reveal the real you. You can be vulnerable, and you can be real. Every interaction you have, every conversation you engage in, is a chance to show yourself and build a real connection.

You build commitment by being transparent and authentic with your people.

Your people want to know who you are before they commit to following you.

If I don't know you, why would I follow you?

WHAT IS COMPLIANCE?

IT LOOKS LIKE:	IT SOUNDS LIKE:	IT FEELS LIKE:
An empty office at 5:01pm every day. People slumped over their desks, wearing their "screen-saver faces". People just going through the motions.	"Sorry, that's not my job." "Friday? That's just not possible." It sounds like a lot of no, no, no!	Hard work. It's demotivating and disheartening.

What's the result of compliance?

If you only have compliance from your team members, you have low trust. As a leader, you will merely have positional power with little real influence. Your people will say and do all the right things in front of you but will show disrespect and disobedience behind your back. This will result in you having to micromanage their performance to achieve acceptable results at best. People will only do the minimum level of work required and nothing more. There will be low engagement and low alignment, resulting in a stagnant workplace with a lack of growth and innovation. Doesn't sound like a great place to work, does it?

Now, let's compare that to commitment.

WHAT IS COMMITMENT?

IT LOOKS LIKE:	IT SOUNDS LIKE:	IT FEELS LIKE:
Commitment looks like purposeful and focussed work. People are smiling, making eye contact and walking with their shoulders back.	"What else is possible?" "How can I help?" "How do we make that happen by Friday?" It sounds like yes, yes, yes!	Belonging to a tribe - purposeful, in flow. Work is no longer work.

What's the result of commitment?

When you gain genuine commitment from your people, there is a high level of trust and loyalty in your team. You gain influence and engagement as a leader with low turnover and low absenteeism. There's personal accountability and self-leadership, which means you can stop micro-managing and start being creative and innovative.

Your team achieves great results and goes above and beyond to not only get the job done but to exceed your expectations. There's excitement, anticipation and agility in the workplace. As a super coach leader, you strive for commitment from each team member.

Watch the signals and ask yourself:

- What do I see?
- What do I hear?
- What do I feel?

Answer truthfully whether you have compliance or commitment, and ask yourself what you can do to gain more commitment from your team members. Are you showing your people the real, authentic you?

In Part 2 of this book, let's get you to:

- Be vulnerable
- Get visible
- Let go of perfection
- Turn up your inner cheerleader
- Embrace the stage
- Tell it like it is
- Take centre position
- Look them in the eye
- Become a storyteller
- Communicate until they mock you

BE VULNERABLE

For a leader to reveal their true self, they need to have the courage to be vulnerable.

The superhero leader prefers to be in their corner office (hiding in the Batcave). When they do have to face their people, they hide behind a firm-branded PowerPoint presentation with figures, projections, matrixes, graphs and other "inspiring" material.

Guess what? Your people don't care about that stuff. What they care about is the person standing in front of them.

There is no room to hide as a leader. My advice is that if you want to hide, don't go into leadership. I've mentored leaders who have shied away from sharing too much of themselves, saying, "It's not about me; it's about the company." But as a leader, it is all about you; not in an egotistical way, not for personal gain or to become a rock star. But as a leader, you believe in something passionately, you want to create change, and to do that, you need your people to follow you. People won't follow you unless they feel connected to you. They need to understand you. To be a super coach, you must open yourself up and be vulnerable.

When I discuss vulnerability with leaders, often the discussion turns to whether it is a sign of weakness or strength. Strong leadership is traditionally viewed as tough, competitive, goal-oriented, rational and linear. But is this always the case? Can't strength be the opposite? Instead of fighting and putting up walls, isn't it strong to let the walls down and have the courage to be vulnerable? Can't strength be associated with collaboration, emotion, passion and empathy?

In her book, *Daring Greatly*, research professor Brené Brown says: "Vulnerability is not weakness, and the uncertainty, risk, and emotional exposure we face every day are not optional. Our only choice is a question of engagement. Our willingness to own and engage with our vulnerability determines the depth of our courage and the clarity of our purpose. The level to which we protect ourselves from being vulnerable is a measure of our fear and disconnection."[8]

To reveal yourself to your people, to be authentic and genuine, you must be vulnerable. The courage to be vulnerable comes from truly knowing yourself, your values, beliefs, purpose and legacy. When you're unsure of yourself, when your self-worth and self-esteem come from the need to be right (that traditional view of strength), you put your superhero mask on for protection. You want to hide the real you. You don't want to be hurt; you don't want people to judge you.

Without your mask, you feel exposed. You fear you'll get taken advantage of. You fear you'll be judged or rejected. This is a huge

---

8   Brown, B. (2015). *Daring Greatly: How the Courage to be Vulnerable Transforms the Way We Live, Love, Parent, and Lead.* Avery Publishing Group.

risk when you have built your confidence on what other people think of you (the superhero identity) instead of what you think of yourself.

I know that when I walk into some organisations, I get the feeling everyone is ready for battle. As a leader, the battles can seem relentless. You feel you must fight for your voice to be heard, fight for resources, fight for recognition, and fight for your team members. You head into meetings wearing your superhero cape and mask because the costume gives you strength. It makes you feel invincible. Now, imagine that everyone else at the leadership table is wearing their costume, too. It's like a scene out *The Avengers* movie.

How does it feel? When everyone is playing the superhero, there is no opportunity to connect. You view one another competitively. It slows everyone down; it stops you from being agile. You can't see the real person under the mask.

To connect and influence, you must remove the mask. You don't need it. Your power comes from your authenticity, by knowing yourself and being yourself. Without the mask, you'll feel lighter, more like you. People will see the real you and connect with you as a leader.

The great thing is that once you become vulnerable, other people will feel safe to do the same. What a different leadership table you'll be sitting at! No more Iron Man having it out with Captain America. When everyone reveals their true selves, you can connect with one another, see one another, really listen to and understand one another. You might have different points of view, but you will use this diversity to create synergy and innovation, not competition.

Now, before you rip off that mask and start sharing your deepest, darkest secrets in the meeting room, let me clarify that being vulnerable doesn't mean you should share *everything* with *everyone* all the time. It's about being true to yourself.

Sometimes, you may not want to share or feel the need to share. There might not be enough trust in the relationship yet, or it might not be the right situation. And that's OK. You can still acknowledge your feelings and beliefs, even if you don't outwardly share them.

Ask yourself:

- Do I feel safe to show my true self?
- What's my intention in sharing my opinion, belief, feelings or story?
- Am I sharing to build trust, connect with and serve others?
- Or am I sharing to prove I'm right and feed my ego?

THE SCALE OF SHARING

Undersharing

Your mask is firmly in place. No one sees anything. People are suspicious of the undersharer; they suspect a hidden agenda and are sceptical about your ability to lead. They feel like they don't know the real you (and they don't!). It's a bit like wanting to tap on someone's chest and ask, "Hello, who's in there?" People will be unable to make an emotional commitment to you as a leader because they don't know who you truly are. There's disconnection and distrust.

Oversharing

We've all known someone in the office who is an oversharer. This leader shares too much too early, and it makes people feel uncomfortable. Oversharing and sharing for all the wrong reasons create doubt about your leadership motives, making you appear self-absorbed and ego driven. *"It's all about me."* The result is the same as undersharing: disconnection and distrust.

Authenticity

Then comes the sweet spot. Authenticity is where you can be open, honest and vulnerable in an appropriate way. The authentic leader isn't afraid to share their true selves, their beliefs and values, but they also don't overshare. What they share is considered, adds value to their team and strengthens their trust. This is where you make a real connection with your people.

"In order for connection to happen, we have to allow ourselves to be seen, really seen."

- BRENÉ BROWN

GET VISIBLE

Superheroes are only seen when they rush in to rescue the person in distress or to fight the villain. If there isn't a crisis, they're nowhere to be found.

You don't see Spider-Man hanging out at the corner coffee shop, or Wonder Woman lifting weights at her local gym. They become invisible. They hide out at their secret lair, not seen by anyone until they are called upon to save the day. Think Batman and his underground Batcave. No one knows where superheroes go or what they do when they're not playing the hero.

As a super coach, you are always on show. You must be seen by your people. No one connects with a leader who is invisible or mysteriously absent. We've all heard rumours about a leader who's never in the office.

Increasing your visibility is about making sure people understand what you do, how you contribute and what makes you unique.

Without visibility, you'll get lost in the crowd and fail to develop your strong, authentic leadership brand.

Think of your leadership as a business. If you don't market, advertise or have any signage out the front, what would happen? You would go out of business. You might be the best at what you do, but if no one knows about you, you won't get any work. It's the same with leadership. You need to market yourself to attract and retain your best people. So, build your leadership brand. Get out there and be seen.

I work with professionals who are at different stages of their careers. I have the privilege of working with young graduates who are at the start of their professional careers, building their presence in their firm and profession. I discuss with them the importance of being visible and creating their authentic leadership brand. I also work with executives. I remember mentoring a leader who reported directly to the CEO. The interesting thing was that even at that stage in his career, we discussed the same thing: how to be visible.

This leader was driven and passionate about his work. He worked crazy hours and put in 100%. However, the feedback he received was that he needed to give more. His reaction? "I'm not sure I have anything left to give."

In this situation, it's not about giving more. It's about being smart with your focus, time and energy. Of course, delivering on your operational goals is vital to your success, but "business as usual" is a given. You can keep your head down and work extremely hard, but if no one knows what you're doing, you and your team won't get the recognition or future opportunities.

WAYS TO INCREASE YOUR VISIBILITY

- **Do work that adds the greatest value**

  Ask yourself: How do I add the most value to this organisation? What am I getting paid to do? What is my expertise? What's my magic? Focus on that. Effectively delegate work to team members and administration staff and get clear on your role. This may require you to extend trust to others and let go of any perfectionist tendencies.

- **Use your voice at every opportunity**

  Speak up in meetings. Demonstrate your knowledge and share your opinions and ideas. Consider the agenda prior to meetings, and think about questions to ask or examples to share. Volunteer to represent your team at company events. Work on your presenting skills and gain more confidence if you need to. Ask to be placed on high-visibility projects.

- **Build connections with influential people**

  Expand your network within your organisation and externally. Build relationships across different departments. Make the time to attend events and have your elevator pitch ready. Speak with your immediate manager regularly. Grow your online connections and contribute to your online community.

- **Participate in learning opportunities**

  Commit to your professional development. Set an example to your team members. Attend internal and external learning sessions and workshops, ask questions, and meaningfully contribute to discussions. Give valuable feedback.

Help others' learning and development – give a webinar, mentor a junior team member, or write a blog post.

What's holding you back?

It may be a lack of confidence that stops you from promoting yourself and your team. This is when you don't have enough self-belief to speak up and acknowledge your hard work and achievements. It may feel safer to keep your head down and stay under the radar.

You may be so busy and overwhelmed with work that you feel you don't have the time to "get out there". It's not a high priority. Or it might be that you fear criticism and judgement from others if you speak up. The old tall poppy syndrome is still alive and well in Australia.

However, increasing your visibility is not about bragging or over-the-top self-promotion. It's about building your personal leadership brand and the reputation of your team so you can be of greater service to others.

Your leadership brand

Your leadership brand tells your story and sets you apart from others. Your brand is the way people see you. It's what you're known for and what you represent.

Your leadership brand is comprised of your ideas, values, expertise and style. To be memorable, it needs to be distinctive, visible and consistent.

"Your brand is what others say about you when you're not in the room."

- JEFF BEZOS

When you create a strong leadership brand, it gives you influence. It opens opportunities for you and the people you lead, allowing you to make a bigger difference and scale up your expertise and ideas. It enables you to gain heartfelt commitment.

As a leader, you need to set yourself apart from the competition. In other words, to lead with influence, you need to sell yourself. To cut through the noise, you need to market your skills and talents through a strong brand.

Be your brand's designer. Don't let it develop by default. Don't hide under a superhero costume. If you don't act now to brand yourself, others will on your behalf. You'll be judged purely by what others say about you. It's up to you to show the world who you are through what you say and do.

Your brand is a personal promise to your people. It tells them what they can expect from you. In a leadership role, you need to keep this promise and exceed expectations to build trust and commitment.

The most important thing to remember is that you must always base your brand on your authentic self. Start with your values, beliefs, purpose, magic and legacy. All the elements we have explored in the last section of the book are needed to create a brand that is congruent with your character and who you are at a roots level.

If you try to build a brand without doing the work on yourself first, and without a deep level of self-awareness, you can destroy the trust others have in you. People can detect when your brand is fake. You may be able to pretend to be someone you're not for a while, but you won't be able to sustain it. It's too hard. Your behaviour will be inconsistent and unpredictable, and you will struggle to live up to the brand you try to portray, letting people down.

Be steadfast and know what you stand for. You must act according to your purpose, strengths and expertise. At some point in your career, people will get to know the real you. This usually happens during a challenging time. It's easy to maintain appearances when the sun is shining, but once the storm hits, your character is exposed. At this point, if your character doesn't match your brand and who you say you are, you will lose the trust of your people and your influence as a leader.

Of course, your brand will evolve. It needs to, because your values and priorities will change. Your personal brand will become more robust and distinctive as you gain greater insight into your purpose and who you are as a leader.

IDEAS TO CREATE YOUR LEADERSHIP BRAND

- **Tell your story.** Authentic storytelling is a huge part of building your brand.
- **Consider what you say yes and no to.** Where you spend your time says a lot about what you value.
- **Your outward appearance impacts your brand.** Be deliberate about how you dress, look, walk and talk.

- **Align your online personality with your brand.** Be consistent with your message on social media and be cautious about what you "like" and share.
- **Let your personality shine.** People want to know the real you. What are your interests outside of work? I've known leaders who love surfing, who are coffee fanatics, who are foodies, who adore their miniature schnauzers or who cycle every day to work. Share these passions with your people.
- **Make every interaction count.** Everything you say and do adds to your brand.

LET GO OF PERFECTION

I know your secret. You're not perfect underneath that cape and mask, are you?

Guess what? I'm not, either. Thank goodness! So, take them off and let your people see the real you, the perfectly imperfect leader.

Superheroes always appear to be perfect. They save the day, every day. Always winning the battle!

In business leadership, it's not like that. You have good days and bad. You have moments that make you proud, and moments that make you wish the ground would open and swallow you whole!

As a leader, you can often feel the pressure to never make mistakes or show weakness. That's some serious stress and anxiety. The burden of perfectionism is a real confidence killer.

Letting go of the idea that you should be great at everything is liberating. Perfectionism is an impossible goal. It's a construct, a script you have read and memorised, a fiction about what you supposedly need to do to succeed and be enough in this world. You might have a script about what it means to be the perfect leader.

Revealing yourself is about amplifying your strengths and acknowledging your weaknesses and flaws. You don't want to dwell on them, but you must acknowledge them, be real about them, and decide how to deal with them.

As a leader, when you stop striving for perfection and say to others honestly, "I actually suck at these things over here, and I'm OK with that," you give them permission to stop judging themselves so harshly. They, too, can take a deep breath and stop striving for perfection. You create a new way for them to measure success and know what it means to be enough. They no longer fear admitting to their flaws; they feel safer taking a risk and know it's OK if they fail. What a gift you can give others: permission to throw out the perfection script!

Acknowledging your weaknesses means you can be comfortable in your skin. You get to be the real you because you're honest and truthful with yourself. Your flaws humanise you, which means you're more approachable as a leader. People will want to commit to you and go above and beyond. Yes, we want leaders to be confident, but real confidence comes from within. Confidence comes from knowing who you are and having a strong, unwavering self-belief. It doesn't come from being perfect or pretending to be perfect.

In fact, if someone seems too perfect at everything, it can create suspicion. Can you really trust someone who is that perfect? It seems too good to be true, and you start to question them. "Is there something they're hiding?" No one commits to a leader if they think they're not showing their true selves.

Great leadership is letting go of the need to be right and to know more than everyone else. It's not about being the best at everything. It's about getting better as a leader.

In one of Seth Godin's recent blog posts, he wrote: "Imperfect is a chance for contribution, connection and improvisation. It's a chance to see the humanity behind the moment you were spending so much energy creating. The alternative to *perfect* might be *better*."[9]

Leadership is being confident enough to ask for help. Your weaknesses are someone else's strengths, and a great leader knows when they need to acknowledge and rely on other people's expertise and knowledge. This, in turn, builds the confidence and skills of those around you.

Above all, leadership is about human connection. It's true; it's not easy to admit to your flaws in the workplace – it takes courage and a degree of vulnerability. But it is worth the risk. You'll create a strong bond with your people and gain a deep commitment from them. Your strengths will give them such value and inspiration that they will forgive your faults or may not even notice them.

If you try to do everything, you may end up doing nothing at all. You will fail to meet deadlines because everything takes more time than it should. You then start feeling like a failure. In your quest for perfection, you end up appearing incompetent, and worse, you won't achieve your goals.

---

9   Godin, S. "Alternatives to perfect", Seth's Blog, 18 May, 2020. https://seths. blog/2020/05/alternatives-to-perfect

Your limitations make room for your talents. Don't dwell on them. Remember, you want to put your energy into your strengths. When you consider a weakness, ask yourself: "Do I have an opposite strength I can build upon?" You see, for every weakness there is often an opposite strength. We all have this dichotomy. Steve Jobs said, "In most cases, strengths and weaknesses are two sides of the same coin. A strength in one situation is a weakness in another, yet often the person can't switch gears."

For example, a leader who has great vision and can see the bigger picture may have a lack of attention to detail. A leader who has an amazing ability to weigh up a situation and analyse a problem may have a pessimistic outlook. A leader who shows empathy and makes strong emotional connections may want harmony in their team at any cost.

As a super coach, switch those negative thoughts into positive ones. Believe in yourself. Otherwise, you might find yourself suffering from the imposter syndrome. This is the persistent fear of being exposed as a fraud in your leadership position. It's that voice in your head that says, "What are you doing here? They're going to find you out!"

Sound familiar? It does to me, and I'm not alone. Researchers believe that up to 70% of people have suffered from imposter syndrome at some point.[10]

Imposter syndrome may take the form of perfectionism: the belief that you need to be perfect at everything to be successful in your role. You discount praise from others and believe your goals have

---

10 Warrell, M. "*Afraid Of Being 'Found Out'? How To Overcome Imposter Syndrome*", Forbes, 3 April, 2014. https://www.forbes.com/sites/margiewarrell/2014/04/03/impostor-syndrome/#6f47b3b348a9

been achieved through sheer luck rather than your own efforts. You constantly worry about not being "enough".

The fear of failure – the fear you will be unable to deliver, disappointing everyone – can be overwhelming. You dwell on your mistakes and failures. Imposter syndrome keeps you in your comfort zone, under the radar. You don't want to be seen in case you are judged negatively by others, so you stay safe and may even sabotage yourself because you don't feel you deserve success.

The key is to acknowledge and embrace these feelings and use them to move forward in your leadership career. Remember, you don't have to be perfect to be a super coach. You just have to strive to be better, always learning.

Every moment spent in a quest for impossible perfection is a missed opportunity to gift the world with your leadership magic. Let go of the need to be perfect. Be your true authentic self.

"You are magnificent beyond measure, perfect in your imperfections, and wonderfully made."

– ABIOLA ABRAMS

TURN UP YOUR INNER CHEERLEADER

Revealing your authentic self takes courage. It also requires a strong, positive belief in who you are. You've got to love who you are to want to share it with the world – loud and proud!

So, how do you feel about yourself? Really?

The most important words you will ever say are the words you say to yourself.

It's that little voice in your head, your inner dialogue, that significantly impacts your level of self-belief.

What stories do you tell yourself? What's the script running through your head? How do you truly feel when you look in the mirror? What limits have you put in place?

You can talk yourself into or out of anything. When you put negative thoughts into your conscious mind, you start to act a certain way. What you think impacts your behaviour, and it's easy only to see the negative side of yourself.

We must challenge our negative thoughts. A study conducted by Michigan State University found that the average person has 80,000 thoughts per day, 80% of which are negative.[11]

We need to change our thinking so we can change the results we get in our lives. Positive thinking results in positive action. We can change the way we see ourselves and gain the confidence to share who we are with our people.

The great news is that we can regain control of our thinking. We have a brilliant goal-seeking part of our brains called the reticular activating system, or RAS for short. We can program our RAS to help us achieve our goals. This part of the brain wants us to be right, so it brings to our attention the things that are important to us and discards everything else. Because we are faced with so much information and noise every day, and we couldn't possibly take it all in, our RAS acts like a filter. We program it, and it filters what we see, then helps guide what we do.

So, when you think something and believe it, you make it come true. You look everywhere for evidence of it, and you find it. It's a self-fulfilling prophecy. Have you ever been guilty of focussing

---

11 Millett, M. "Challenge your negative thoughts", Extension, Michigan State University, 31 March, 2017. http://msue.anr.msu.edu/news/challenge_your_negative_thoughts

only on the negative? A million things could have happened in your day, but you focus on the one thing that didn't go so well, the one thing you might have done wrong. That's the way you've programmed your RAS.

Let's say you think you're not the best person for a new leadership position. If this is the way you think, you behave correspondingly. You may not speak up at the next managers' meeting. You may not put the time into the application process. You might even share your negative thoughts with your colleagues, and then you start reading into their behaviour to confirm your beliefs. Suddenly, the email that was missed by your general manager means she doesn't value your work, which means you're not important enough, which means she doesn't want you to get the leadership position. And guess what happens next? You don't get the job. You were right. You thought it, you put energy into it, your focus was purely on the negative, then bingo – that's what you got.

Thought -> energy -> manifestation

Your thoughts are more powerful than you think. Thankfully, your thoughts are in your circle of control. You get to choose your thinking and, importantly, how you think about yourself.

Have you ever allowed your negative self-judgement to impact your influence as a leader? Have you ever been in a meeting and wanted to ask a question or make a comment, but before you opened your mouth, you told yourself, "Just be quiet, that's a stupid question, no one wants to hear your opinion." Maybe you've thought about writing something like a blog or an article and, again, all you hear is, "Who are you to be writing something like that? Who's going to read it? Best not to do anything at all."

This is your self-judgement hard at work. It stops you from sharing your thoughts and ideas. It discourages you from stepping outside your comfort zone and taking a risk.

In my job, I write content every day: blogs, webinars, training programs, social media posts, keynote presentations... the list goes on. I've been doing this gig for a while now, but at times I still find myself hindered by my own harsh self-judgement.

I'm sure all of us can admit to self-judging to some extent. Self-judgement comes from our internal messages based on our experience and history. It impacts the way we view ourselves and, unfortunately, can have a negative, harsh and over-critical voice: our inner-critic.

If we can let go of our critical self-judgement, we can:

- Follow our passion
- Make a more meaningful contribution
- Grow and learn
- Be creative
- Be vulnerable

So, how can we deal with this self-judgement?

Let's think of self-judgement as a knock at your front door.

1. Firstly, you become aware that someone is at your front door. So, what does it sound like? It might be a small knock, or it might be someone ringing the doorbell incessantly. How do you feel when you hear this? Maybe there's a tightness in your chest, perhaps your breath quickens. What are the red flags when self-judgement comes knocking?
2. Secondly, answer the door by opening it slightly. Leave it ajar and see who's there. Often, there are two people: your

inner critic at the front, taking up the most room and being assertive; and your inner cheerleader, standing patiently at the back, waiting to be heard.

3. Only let in your inner cheerleader, that part of your self-judgement that's positive, encouraging, wise, loving, and respectful. Then quickly shut the door.

As you start to only let in compassion, acceptance and self-belief, your script starts to change. You'll find your inner critic gets smaller, quieter, and may stop showing up at your door altogether.

You can transform your limiting beliefs into useful, motivating ones. Beliefs that are authentic and show the real you. Every time you recite those positive beliefs, you reaffirm and strengthen them. They will bring about positive action because you make it so much easier for your RAS to see evidence that supports your belief.

As a leader, there are so many people judging you; you don't need to be one of them. It's time to give yourself a break. Be kind to yourself so you can do the work you are meant to do.

Super coach leadership is about creating change and enabling growth. Don't let your self-judgement hold you back from making your contribution and revealing who you are. It's important to have your cheerleader by your side.

"Whether you think you can, or you think you can't, you're right."

– HENRY FORD

EMBRACE
THE STAGE

As a leader, all eyes are on you. People are watching you. They're waiting for your response and reaction. They're observing what you do, listening to what you say, and noticing the language you use.

They're picking up on your non-verbal cues, too: your tone of voice, eye contact and body language. They look for clues for what you believe in, your values, and who you are as a leader.

When I'm in a team meeting, I always notice when something controversial is shared. Everyone immediately looks to their leader to see how she or he reacts. Was that a shrug or a nod? What do the crossed arms mean? Was that a smirk?

I once had a manager who, whenever he didn't agree with something being said or was starting to get impatient, would lean back on his chair and place his hands behind his head. The whole team knew what it meant, and whenever it happened, we knew we had to wrap up the meeting quickly.

What are your cues?

What messages do you (possibly unintentionally) send to your team?

What impact does this have on your people and their level of commitment?

A few months ago, I was on a plane going to a legal conference. For those of you who know me well, you know I like to talk! So, if I'm on a plane and the person sitting next to me is up for a chat, I'm all in.

On this flight, as soon as I sat down, the guy next to me started asking me questions – where was I going, what did I do for work – and we ended up talking for the whole two-hour flight. We talked about business, our careers, our beliefs, and what we loved about our work. It was such a great conversation and time just flew by (pardon the pun).

I arrived at the conference later that afternoon and attended a couple of sessions. That night, there were welcome cocktail drinks (always my favourite part of any conference!). One of my colleagues grabbed me and introduced me to the managing partner of a national law firm.

She said to him "You should really meet Midja." And he replied, "Yes. I feel like I already know Midja." I asked, "Have we met before?" And he said, "No, but I was sitting in the seat in front of you on the plane this morning. I was going to put my headphones on, but when I started to listen to your conversation, I was intrigued and just kept listening."

Oh, my goodness! We both started to laugh. Well, his was a laugh, mine was more like a nervous giggle as I tried to remember everything that came out of my mouth during that two-hour flight! Sometimes I have a lot to say!

This was a reminder for me that you never know who's watching and listening. Therefore, at all times, you must choose your words carefully while remaining true to yourself. You need to be clear on what you want to share, and consider the impact your words and actions have on others. I was always told that when you talk about someone else, imagine that person is standing right there beside you.

When you're a leader, you're always on stage. A super coach embraces this stage and uses it to reveal who they are and what they believe in. This is one way they gain commitment from their people.

I attended a leadership course many years ago at the Disney Institute in Florida. The course was amazing, as you would expect from Disney, and the presenters talked about the Disney philosophy of "on stage/off stage". Off stage, the cast members (the title given to Disney employees) arrive for work, dress in their uniform, take breaks, eat, and interact with each other away from the view of the guests. When they enter the park and move on stage, they are immaculately dressed, smiling, and ready to create the very best experience for their guests.

Just like Disney's cast members, as a leader, you're responsible for making the experience in your workplace the best. You're responsible for your people's level of commitment.

Every time you step into the office, attend a conference, see a client or even catch a plane (!), you're on stage. There's no hiding as a leader. Every time you talk about yourself, your business, your people or your clients, do so in a way you would be happy for anyone to hear.

"When we are on stage, we are in the here and now."

– CONSTANTIN STANISLAVSKI

TELL IT LIKE IT IS

L et's call him Rob. Online, Rob is 47 years old, single, an entrepreneur, likes to keep fit, and has dark hair, a beard and piercing green eyes. I like.

Fast forward to meeting Rob for a drink.

Hmm... Rob is 59 years old, currently not working but thinking of starting his own business, pays for a gym membership, and his relationship status is "it's complicated". And let's just say that Rob's photos were taken before there was such a thing as online dating!

Why, Rob? Why?

Now, I understand that Rob might be trying to get "an interview" – a foot in the door, so to speak. But he's got to know that, at some point, I'm going to find out the truth.

Honesty matters. Always.

So, let's be honest with each other. Tell me:

- Who are you?
- What do you stand for as a leader?
- What's it like to work with you?
- What can I expect from you?
- What do you expect from me?

And, for goodness' sake, just give it to me straight!

Honesty builds commitment. If you want me to follow you as a leader, if you want me to do my very best work for you, to commit to you and your future vision, then I have to trust you. As a leader, you must have the courage to put yourself out there, show yourself and tell the truth.

Your honesty will build a culture of open communication, transparency and safety. Your people will know they can trust what you say and that they, too, can share honestly and openly.

If you've done the work on discovering who you are, your strengths, your story, and the things that make you unique, then tell it like it is. Share who you truly are with your people. What are your opinions and thoughts? What's great about working with you and your team?

Be real. Don't tell me you're a highly collaborative leader if you prefer to work autonomously. Don't tell me that this is an innovative role if it's highly process driven with little room for creativity.

People know when you're faking it. Just like Rob, you may be able to get away with it for a while, but people will discover the truth. People can see through the BS. They can tell when they're only being told one part of the story.

The super coach isn't tempted to tell people only what they want to hear. They know deception breaks trust, damages their reputation and wastes everyone's time and energy. Do you really want to keep up a charade? Saying one thing when you mean another is exhausting and a lot of hard work. It's also a slippery slope. Once you tell one lie, you need to tell another and another, until you're way over your head in deceit and deception.

Now, sometimes honesty isn't always pleasant, and it might be the case that initially, your people don't take the news well. But honesty is always the best policy (this saying has stood the test of time for a good reason). A little white lie every now and then about a not-so-great outfit or haircut might be OK, but when it comes to the things that matter, honesty is critical. It builds your integrity and strengthens your reputation.

As a leader, you want to attract the right people for your organisation – people who share your beliefs and commit to your vision. You won't find those people unless you represent yourself and your organisation truthfully.

Jack Welch, former CEO of General Electric, calls it candour as a leader. In his book, *Winning*, he writes:

"A remarkable absence of candour in the workplace represents one of the most significant obstacles to companies' success. In a bureaucracy, people are afraid to speak out. This type of environment slows you down, and it doesn't improve the workplace." [12]

We expect honesty first and foremost from our leaders, and it is the most valued leadership quality by far. [13]

---

12 Welch, J. (2005). *Winning*. HarperCollins.
13 Kouzes, J. and Posner, B. (2017). *The Leadership Challenge: How to Make Extraordinary Things Happen in Organizations.* John Wiley and Sons Ltd.

Your people want to know who you are. They want a leader who ditches the mask and dares to show themselves, flaws and all.

Don't be like Rob. Tell it like it is.

Don't expect loyalty when you can't provide honesty.

TAKE CENTRE POSITION

Recently, I coached a leader who had received some off-the-cuff comments from his team members. He'd walked into a meeting and one of his team members said, "Hello, stranger." Ouch!

Another senior leader commented to me a few years ago that when he walked into the room at an annual firm event, people gasped. They were so shocked to see him in the flesh.

As a leader, if you get these reactions from your people, it's time to re-think your priorities.

Leadership is a contact sport.

You've got to be in there, getting dirty.

It's not about putting on a superhero costume, catching a lift to the top floor, walking into a corner office and shutting the door. Super coaches are comfortable with getting up close and personal with their people.

Face time in business is priceless. The word "company", as in "companion", comes from the Latin word "panis", meaning "to share bread".[14] The daily luncheon habit of US oil industry magnate John D. Rockefeller is described in the biography, *Titan*. Every day, Rockefeller would sit down with his people, have lunch and talk. This was how he built strong, sustainable relationships.[15]

To succeed as a leader, we've spoken about how important commitment is from your people. Without it, you'll fail to deliver results to your clients. Your people need to be willing to go the extra mile. You need to persuade, inspire and influence, and you can't do this through a computer screen or telephone. Revealing yourself as a leader and who you are needs face time.

As a mentor and facilitator, I sometimes work with my clients on the phone or via Skype, but nothing beats the connection I make when I'm face-to-face with a client, either one-on-one or in a workshop setting. When we can see one another, when we can see each other's faces, reactions and body language, we can genuinely engage with one another. When we're face-to-face with someone, our "mirror neurons" mimic the other person's behaviours, sensations, feelings and energy. Our brains love it. Rapport is quickly established, and communication is easy.

I know life can get hectic, and it's easy for relationships in the office to become transactional. You can forget to make time for your

---

14 "Breaking Bread with 'Companion'", ," Merriam-Webster. https://www. merriam-webster.com/words-at-play/history-of-word-companion
15 Chernow, R. (2004). *Titan: The Life of John D. Rockefeller, Sr.* Random House

people or postpone that meeting for another day. The result? Your people disengage, disconnect, and stop performing at their best.

It's time to lead from centre position.

In 2010, I attended a learning and development conference in Orlando, Florida, called Learning 2010. My colleague and good friend Debbie and I had been invited to speak about our firm's residential training facility and the courses we designed and facilitated. It was a fantastic opportunity, and one of my all-time favourite experiences.

On the second day of the conference, we headed out for our lunch break and enjoyed a meal with our fellow delegates, not knowing what was going on inside the auditorium. We were soon to find out. When we opened the doors to commence the afternoon session, we were shocked. During the lunch break, the entire Orlando Philharmonic Orchestra had set up in the middle of the room and started playing! The beautiful sound resonated around the auditorium.

The conductor of the orchestra was Roger Nierenberg, author of the leadership book, Maestro: A Surprising Story About Leading by Listening. *Roger invited us to hear the orchestra from out in front, where the conductor traditionally stands. He then asked us to experience what it was like to listen from the middle of the orchestra. What a different feeling! A richer, stronger sound. I felt more connected, like I was part of the music.*

Leadership is a lot like conducting an orchestra.

As a leader, you can spend all your time out the front of your people, waving your hands around, giving directions. A little more of this, a little less of that. Of course, guidance and instructions are needed in leadership, but what are also required are connection, understanding and knowledge of what is actually happening in the business, not just what's written in the latest board report.

How do you experience these things? How do you give and receive information? You need to get amongst it, get in the centre. From the centre, you'll gain a different perspective. You'll be closer to the business processes, the clients, and, of course, your people. From the centre, you can easily access every part of the business and everyone in it. People can see the real you from every angle, and you can see them. It's like a theatre in the round – the actors have nowhere to hide, and every audience member gets a view of the performance. Similarly, every team member deserves to see you and know the real you. Give them that opportunity.

If you never get amongst your people, you can lose perspective of what's going on in your team. You lose touch with reality. You get caught up in the executive hype and talk the good talk: "We have strong cultural alignment with our values, we have a dedicated and motivated workforce…" Blah, blah, blah. All the rhetoric in the world. You can get caught up in your own management report and start believing it. You rely on your superhero power, become completely task oriented, and forget about truly connecting with your people, who are your greatest asset.

TIPS:

- **Get out of the top-floor corner office and be seen**

  Engage in conversations. Ask questions and listen. Usually, the more senior the leader, the further away they are physically from their people and the "hub" of the business. At my old firm, the managing partner and I would often sit and have a cuppa in the kitchen. It was amazing how much he heard and what he learnt from the people coming in and out of the lunchroom, talking away, not even noticing the managing partner was sitting at one of the tables.

- **Make time to attend events**

  Turn up to other team meetings and events – for example, a celebratory morning tea, induction training for new staff or a lunchtime webinar. At first, people might be shocked to see you. They might even be a little anxious or concerned. You must be open and honest about your intention for attending. It might take a little while to create a new cultural norm.

- **Bring your people physically together**

  When you're meeting, training and learning with others, it's not just the formal discussion in the room that's valuable. It's also the conversations you have at morning tea or lunch. This is where the real magic can happen. You engage in a conversation with someone that sparks a new way of thinking, and you build relationships with people you would never have met otherwise.

  Sure, webinars, Skype meetings, emails and e-learning have their place. They are wonderful tools to connect people with just-in-time learning concepts and compliance training, and they help managers stay connected when they are geographically dispersed. However, when it comes to cultural alignment, leadership development, behavioural change and inspirational connection, you need to bring your people together. Those things can't happen over a screen.

- **Discover the client experience**

  Get up close and personal with your clients. Get out into the trenches. Find out what their problems are and how they're feeling. Ask questions. Get curious. Attend a client meeting or site inspection, whatever you can do to connect with your clients and understand their needs.

LOOK THEM
IN THE EYE

My youngest son, Jack, is nine years old. He has some interesting quirks, as we all do. However, one thing he did when he was younger always reminded me of what it takes to be a great leader.

As a mum, I say a lot of things on the fly. And, as a leader, I do exactly the same thing.

"That report – sure, I'll have a read of it today."

"Friday's meeting – yes, I'll be there."

"Approval for that training session – consider it done."

Busy, busy, busy. Making promises and setting expectations. All good, right? Well, it's all good unless you don't follow through.

When Jack was younger, he wouldn't let me get away with not following through. Whenever I made an off-the-cuff promise to him as I was hanging out the washing or making dinner, he would stop me, turn me around to look at him, and point into his eyes. He would say, "Look at me. Look at me, Mum. Now promise." I would have to stop, look him in the eye, and promise. (Reminds of me Kim in *Kath & Kim* – "look at moi, look at moi!")

Every time, Jack did this, he made me stop to consider the commitment I was about to make. You see, one of the most important things you can do as a leader (and as a parent) is to keep the promises you make to your people. Making a promise to someone is one of the most powerful forms of communication.

Yet how often do you make a promise you can't possibly keep?

Why do we break our promises?

No doubt you have the best of intentions. When you made the promise, you honestly thought you would be able to deliver, but you got busy or distracted, or other priorities got in the way, and you let the promise go. You think, "Ah well, it was only something small, I'll get around to it. I'm sure they'll understand." But will they?

Maybe you hope your bold promise to meet a deadline will force you and your team to work harder to deliver beyond what you think you're capable of.

Maybe you're uncomfortable saying no and want to please others. You don't want to let the team down, so you make the promise to keep the peace, but then you fail to follow through.

The impact of failing to follow through is disastrous – on your relationships and reputation. Remember, your word is your reputation. By not keeping your promise, you become known as someone who can't be counted on. It disappoints your team and erodes your self-esteem.

Trust dissolves when promises are broken and future agreements no longer hold weight. That's why it's so important to slow down, be present with your people, and consider the impact before you make a promise. I'm not saying this is easy. It can be tough, particularly in this age of distraction. But it's critical you look your people in the eye and only promise what you know you will deliver.

As a super coach:

- Slow down.
- Understand your priorities and workload. What can you realistically do and by when?
- Talk straight to your people. Speak the truth and choose your words carefully when making a promise.
- Keep a record of your commitments and make this record visible. Visibility leads to action.
- If plans change, offer an explanation as soon as possible. Set a new way forward.
- Learn how to say "no" or "not now" in a way that contributes to the relationship and makes it stronger.

Leaders with good intentions make promises.

Leaders with good character keep them.

BECOME A
STORYTELLER

Storytelling is one of the most powerful ways to reveal who
you are, what you stand for as a leader, and your vision
for your team.

People have been telling stories since the dawn of time.
Strong cultures throughout history have shared their
beliefs and values through stories, some of which have become
legends passed from generation to generation by their leaders.
If you want to build commitment, make storytelling part of your
leadership toolkit.

"We have stories to tell, stories that provide wisdom about the journey of life. What more have we to give one another than our 'truth' about human adventure as honestly and as openly as we know how?"

RABBI SAUL RUBIN

I once mentored a client who was a chief financial officer. She had always worked in finance and loved the numbers game.

One day, she shared with me a story from her childhood. She remembers being with her mum, walking past a dress shop. Her mum looked longingly through the window, wanting to buy the dress, but just couldn't afford it. My client said it was now important to her that if a woman saw something she really wanted, she needed the financial independence to buy it. To my client, it's all about financial freedom, cashflow, budgeting and smart decision making.

After hearing this story, there was no doubt in my mind why this leader did what she did. It made clear the vision she had for her career and the impact she wanted to make. No qualifications, job experience or list of impressive clients could have told me more than that one simple yet powerful story. I felt like I knew her.

When you give people instructions and information in a standard way – e.g. by telling them what is right or wrong and what you want them to do – it's often filed away, never to be retrieved again. They may have some fleeting interest in what you're saying, but there is no change in their knowledge or behaviours. They have no meaningful connection with what you're saying.

However, people react to stories and narrative in an entirely different way. We process stories through immersion – by putting ourselves in the story. We ask ourselves what we would do in the situation, calling on our own ideas and experience, and making the story something we can relate to. That's why storytelling creates lasting changes of opinion and knowledge.

As a leader, you can tell stories to illustrate desired behaviours, explain your values, share a lesson, clarify your strategic goals or describe a vision. Storytelling has so many benefits.

Firstly, stories humanise you as a leader. They build commitment and connection. Your stories reveal who you are, connecting you with your people, transmitting information and your personal experience. Your people have a genuine interest in knowing who you are and where you have come from.

Many times, I have been part of a company's strategy day or induction process. The number-one question asked of the CEO is, "Tell me your story. How did you become the leader you are today?"

Secondly, you can use stories to convey concepts or ideas that might otherwise be difficult to articulate, such as a complicated process. Stories help simplify and clarify our thoughts.

Most importantly, stories inspire others to act. Leaders are often concerned about what they want to tell people or how they want to tell people something. But your first question should be, "How do I want to make them feel?" Stories that evoke imagination and emotion can be highly persuasive. We remember what we feel.

And, let's face it, stories are fun. Would you rather tell someone about your vision and what you stand for as a leader, or show them through a story? Telling people is not motivating. But a story that makes people join the dots and experience that real "a-ha" moment is powerful. By allowing your people to unpack the story themselves, you make a lasting impact. You pull people in rather than push your message, and you invite them to come along for the journey and participate.

Storytelling tips

- **Check your intention for telling a story**

  Do you want to reveal a genuine part of yourself, build trust, connect people, share a lesson learnt or impart knowledge? (All great reasons.) Or do you want to manipulate others or make yourself look good? If that's the case, you might end up doing the opposite.

- **Bring your story to life by evoking all the senses**

  What did you see, hear, feel, smell and taste? Immerse your people in the experience and paint a picture. Take them on a journey. In *The Hero with a Thousand Faces*, author Joseph Campbell describes the idea of a monomyth, an archetypal narrative structure that outlines the hero's journey. The hero's journey starts with an ordinary person who experiences a call to adventure. Then there is a three-part structure comprised of the departure or challenge, the action and transformation, and finally the return. This structure gives stories a simple yet powerful framework. Each story needs conflict and resolution, tension and release, mystery and revelation. There must be losses and triumphs, peaks and troughs.

- **Take time to craft your stories and practise them**

  Make your stories compelling. I always giggle when people hear a speaker and say what a wonderful, natural storyteller they are. Of course, they might be a natural, but chances are they have also spent a lot of time and energy crafting and practising the right delivery. They have received feedback on their stories and reworked them.

- **Ensure there is simplicity in your story**

  Choose your words carefully. No one wants a long-winded version. There is an art to including just enough detail to set the scene and evoke emotion without cluttering your story and losing your audience. Every sentence must add to the story.

- **Take care to select the right story**

  Tell it at the right time to the right audience. Stories about failing and learning from your mistakes pull people in. Stories that serve only to self-promote turn people away.

- **Tell the truth, the whole truth**

  If you leave the bad bits out of the story, you create distrust. You need to be vulnerable with your storytelling and have the courage to tell your truth. It's the pain people will learn from the most.

- **Make your stories relatable**

  People want to feel you have experienced their problems, pain and fear. They also want to know how you overcame them. Stories that feel familiar – *"I've been there, too"* – are the most powerful because they're relatable. The audience can imagine themselves in the story, being the hero of their own journey, and they are more likely to connect with you and remember what you're saying.

"There is no greater power on this earth than story."

– LIBBA BRAY

COMMUNICATE UNTIL THEY MOCK YOU

O f all the leadership responsibilities, communication is the most powerful and enduring – especially in times of challenge and disruption. If you can get it right, you'll connect with and inspire your people to go above and beyond.

Communication is so much more than the transmission of information. The messages you communicate reveal a lot about who you are and your leadership priorities. You must understand your audience when you deliver a message, so it hits the mark and gets the desired result.

Consider:

- What is your message, and how will you say it?
- What is your mode of communication – words, tone of voice, facial expressions, and body language?
- How do you project yourself to others?
- Do they see you as a confident and optimistic leader?

A super coach communicates openly with their team, knowing transparency builds commitment.

Show your people you have nothing to hide. Be authentic in your communication style and willing to reveal more of yourself so your people can see the real you.

Time is also of the essence. It's essential you communicate important messages as quickly as possible. The last thing you want people in your team to do is play the game of Chinese whispers. Rumours can spread rapidly. If you don't communicate important information or key decisions promptly, your people will fill in the gaps with their assumptions. Doubt, speculation and suspicion will run rife instead of trust, commitment and collaboration.

Consistency is key. As a leader, it's easy to assume that if you say something once, your people will remember and act on it. This assumption can get you into trouble. If you have children, you'll understand what I mean! I often find myself saying, "How many times do I have to tell you to (insert instructions here)?" If I ask my teenage daughter to clean her room or put her dirty clothes in the laundry, do you think she does it the first time? Not a chance.

I was once advised by a well-respected mentor that, as a leader, I should communicate my message until people start to mock me. In other words, until they begin to laugh, roll their eyes like they know what's going to come out of my mouth next, and say things like, "Oh well, here she goes again."

You see, it's only at the point where your people start to mock you that you know they've taken your message on board. Your message has permeated into the culture of your team, and it's now part of the common language. You can then take a step back and decrease the frequency of your communication because your people will start to act on your messages. They'll be your message ambassadors, with your messages front of mind, influencing their decisions and actions every day.

In an organisation I once worked for, we had a set of three values that were communicated at every opportunity: in meetings, training sessions, performance appraisals, staff awards, and on the intranet. They were also part of all firm policies, manuals and performance criteria. These values were communicated everywhere – I'll be able to recite them for the rest of my life!

Your key messages need to be front of mind so your people act on them. You want to ensure your messages are programmed into their reticular activating system (RAS). As we talked about in the section - Turn Up Your Inner Cheerleader, the RAS acts as a filter for our brains. It makes certain things a part of conscious thought, and you want your key messages to be part of your people's conscious thinking. You want them to keep coming back to those messages in their everyday interactions with clients and other team members. They must fully understand what is expected of them.

The impact of this type of communication is that you'll get the behaviours and results you want. And, as your people grow and develop, they'll take something different from your messages. They'll adapt their understanding depending on what's happening to them at that time, their own growth and development, and their specific needs. How many times have you read or heard something once, taken a couple of key points away, then a year or two later, you've come back to the same message and had a slightly different interpretation? Your people will do the same with your key messages.

If you make the mistake of thinking you can communicate something once and your people will immediately understand and act on it, you'll end up frustrated and disappointed. At some point, you'll realise you've been on different wavelengths. You're not getting what you asked for, and key goals are not being met. You're just not understood.

You might shy away from repeating your message because you feel you're nagging people. Let's face it, no one wants to be labelled a nag. But without repeating your message, it won't stick. What you must do is get creative with how you deliver your message. How can you deliver your message multiple times through different media to get it across? Think about what you can do in face-to-face communications, through emails, the intranet, in meetings, and the stories you tell.

So, how much is enough? How many times do you need to communicate your message? Advertising research indicates that people show a preference for an idea or message if they are familiar with it. This is called the mere-exposure effect, a term coined by psychologist Robert Zajonc. It means that repeating a message more than once leads to familiarity with that message, which then leads to a preference for it. Studies have shown that mere exposure reaches its maximum impact between 10 and 20 exposures. After that, the effectiveness declines.[16]

---

16 Relojo, D. "How Do Companies Use the Mere-Exposure Effect to Attract Customers?" Psychreg, 28 December, 2017. https://www.psychreg.org/mere-exposure-effect

Ideas to ensure your messages have maximum impact:

- **Determine your big messages.** For example, your vision statement, mission, values, key client behaviours, team charter, sayings and quotes that epitomise your key beliefs.
- **Be proactive and strategic with your communication.** Create and implement a communication plan.
- **Weave your messages into your storytelling.** Explain the why behind your messages.
- **Get in front of your people.** Convey your messages in everyday conversations.
- **Be mindful of your non-verbal cues.** Your facial expressions and body language can affect what you want to convey.
- **Look for opportunities to put your messages in written form.** For example, the employee handbook, emails, intranet and training documents.
- **Add a personal touch to your messages.** Show your personality and find your authentic voice.
- **Consider using video to send messages**, particularly to your remote working team members. Video builds a stronger connection and commitment.
- **And just when you think they've got it, say it again!**

"The single biggest problem in communication is the illusion that it has taken place."

– GEORGE BERNARD SHAW

Part 3

EMPOWER

A superhero works alone and takes all the glory.

A super coach works with others and shares responsibility and recognition.

EMPOWER YOUR PEOPLE TO BUILD TRUST

A superhero loves the spotlight. They singlehandedly fight the villain, save the girl and restore peace to the city. They work alone – well, maybe with a sidekick at times, but mostly alone. They are in control and call the shots, and they also take all the glory.

A super coach wants to build collaboration and empower their people. A super coach discovers and reveals themselves, then forgets about themselves. Their focus shifts to their people. They want to be in service to their team and see them succeed.

"Before you become a leader, success is all about growing yourself. When you become a leader, success is all about growing others."

– JACK WELCH

I once worked with a leader who was passionate about her job. She was a perfectionist, driven and dedicated, which, of course, are all great qualities. But the flip side was that she was overprotective of her ideas and micromanaged her people, and it was hard to get anything out of her department. She wanted to make every decision and check every piece of work herself. There was no doubt she acted this way because she cared so much about the work and wanted everything to be perfect. But although her intention was good, her impact wasn't.

Something needed to change. Otherwise, this leader was going to burn out. Her leadership brand was suffering; she was working long hours but getting negative feedback. However, this feedback gave her the opportunity to consider the responsibility and accountability of her team members. She realised she was scared to let go. "What if something goes wrong?" she asked me.

The fear of something going wrong, the fear of failure, can hold you back from empowering your people. As a leader, you need to make sure you have the right people doing the right things in the right way. You simply don't have the time or headspace to make every single decision for your team.

When you empower your people to make their own decisions, it frees your time. You can focus on strategy and the areas where you add the most value. Furthermore, each team member gets more clarity on their role and level of authority. It gives them a path for career progression, which can help you with succession planning.

When I'm in a leadership role, I like to ask my people:

"What would you do if I wasn't here? What decision would you make?"

By asking these two questions, you step out of the role of superhero and into the role of super coach.

If you retain all the decision-making power, you will continue to micromanage your people. You'll make them dependent on you. This might secretly be what you want, but it doesn't allow them to learn and make mistakes, and you won't find out what they're capable of achieving. It holds your talented people back from making the impact they could make. It also covers up unsatisfactory performance.

Of course, the risk of empowering your people is that things might not get done your way. Perhaps they won't get done at all, or your people will fail. But they're the risks that you, as a leader, must take.

Furthermore, micromanagement costs money. According to a *Harvard Business Review* analysis, US companies waste more than $3 trillion on excess bureaucracy and management every year.[17]

---

17 Hamel, G. and Zanini, M. "Excess Management Is Costing the U.S. $3 Trillion Per Year", Harvard Business Review, 5 September, 2016. https://hbr.org/2016/09/excessmanagement-is-costing-the-us-3-trillion-per-year

Empowering your people makes your team agile and fast. It increases creativity and innovation because you allow new, fresh ideas and approaches to the work.

Most importantly, empowering your team builds **trust**, which is one of the most important ingredients in any relationship, personally or professionally. As a leader, without trust, you'll never create a high-performing team. They'll say one thing to your face because you're the boss, but say something different behind your back, or at least think it. They'll cruise at work, stay under the radar and do what's expected of them, but they'll never go above and beyond.

Let's face it, at times, the corporate environment can feel like a battlefield: office politics and alliances, people scrambling for power, position plays, constant change and uncertainty, and hyper competition. People can feel like they are in the trenches day in, day out. What they need is a leader who they trust; a leader who they believe in and who they know believes in them.

Trust goes two ways. You need to extend trust to receive it in return.

In this busy corporate world, I don't know about you, but I don't have the time or the energy to second guess my people. I don't want to have to micromanage them. I don't want to have to check whether what they've told me is true. What a waste!

I want to trust my people and them to trust me. Only then can we get on with doing the job, delivering to our clients, being creative and innovative, and having some fun along the way!

So, tell me, how do you build trust each day with your people?

In this part, let's get you to:

- Let go of being right
- Seek to understand
- Ask for help
- Engage in conversations that matter
- Give up control
- Discover their talent
- Not forget your middle children
- Know when to hold 'em
- Get them through the boring, boring, boring
- For goodness' sake, have some fun

LET GO OF BEING RIGHT

Being right feels good, doesn't it? It makes you feel confident, worthy and valuable. It makes you feel like a superhero.

As a leader, you have strong ideas and opinions based on your years of experience and vast industry knowledge. You know your stuff. You want to share this knowledge, and you genuinely believe your approach to problem-solving is right. But, of course, it's only *your* way, not *the* way. This can sometimes be difficult to accept.

If you think you're right about everything and always go with your own ideas, your people will eventually stop thinking for themselves. Why would they bother to think creatively and share their points of view when they are never listened to or considered? They will quickly learn their opinions are not valued.

You must allow your viewpoint to be challenged. You also need to be open to changing your mind about a situation. This can be perceived as a weakness in a leader, but it actually demonstrates the opposite. When you're secure and confident enough, you can admit when you're wrong.

"Faced with the choice between changing one's mind and proving that there is no need to do so, almost everyone gets busy on the proof."

– JOHN GALBRAITH

Super coaches don't feel threatened when their opinions are challenged. They're the first ones to say, "I hadn't thought about it that way. Let's give it a try." And when you let go of being right, you genuinely value feedback and can leverage the diversity in your team.

I remember I was once engaged in a conversation with the in-house counsel at a law firm. I discussed the idea of doing after-case reviews with the in-house counsel, the solicitors involved, and the paralegals or any other staff who had worked on the case. I outlined the concept of conducting an informal meeting around what worked well and what we would do differently next time. I said, "So, the great thing about this is, it will give us an opportunity to learn from one another – for the lawyers and paralegals to learn, and for yourself as in-house counsel to learn as well."

The in-house counsel looked at me and said, "What do you mean? There'd be nothing I could learn from one of the junior lawyers." I looked at him, expecting him to laugh like it was a joke. But he didn't. He was dead serious that, as in-house counsel and a senior practitioner, he would have nothing to learn from the solicitor who briefed him.

What a missed opportunity! No matter how senior we are, no matter what's written on our business card, we can always learn from others. That's one of the traits of a super coach. They're open to learning from others, and they value the differences others bring to the discussion.

Now, I must admit, when I started in a leadership position, I struggled to genuinely value the differences of the people in my team. I was naturally drawn to people who thought and acted like me. Those were the people I wanted to work with. They behaved the way I did, and they agreed with me on everything. This is what is known as the Similar-To-Me affect and it is a form of perceptual bias.

Then there were people in the team who were not the same as me. They slowed me down, challenged my ideas, and behaved in a very different way to me. To be honest, for a long time, these people annoyed me! I tolerated them but did I value them? Absolutely not. If I had my way, I would have taken them off my team and replaced them with people like me.

Now when I admit that, it makes me shudder. What was I thinking? A bunch of mini Midjas? What a disaster!

As leaders, we need people around us who are different to us – people who behave differently, see things differently and complement our skill set. Of course, you want to have a shared vision and robust set of aligned values and beliefs, but when it comes to how you work, you want the people in your team to be different. It will be those differences that make your team truly special.

To empower your team, let go of being right. Value their opinions. You need to be genuinely open to having your opinions changed and see the world through their eyes. You'll be surprised how your team steps up when they realise it's not always your way.

A BEER, A SONG AND A LEADER

Last year, I went to my first pub choir in Brisbane. It was such a great night! I don't know if you've ever been to a pub choir, but if not, I highly recommend it.

So, what is it? It's an event where a few hundred people who don't know each other come together in a pub for 90 minutes and perform a song in three-part harmony. On a Wednesday night, we sang the classic 1980s song, "Everybody Wants To Rule The World", by English band Tears for Fears, and it was such a fabulous experience that I've already booked my ticket for the next event.

As I stood there in the pub, I thought about this choir and its connection with leadership. When you bring people together like that, it's a wonderful example of collaboration and synergy: a group of people who want to connect with one another, who have something in common, and want to be a part of something bigger than themselves. They create something they can't create by themselves. And, as a leader, that's exactly what you want in your team.

Our leader was the amazing and highly talented Astrid Jorgensen. She stood up on the stage, giving us direction, showing us the way and making us laugh. She was focussed on the task at hand and obviously highly experienced.

One part of the night during rehearsals really struck a chord with me. Astrid broke down the song for us and sang a section, then asked us to repeat it back to her. There was one particular set of notes she sang, but when she asked us to sing it back to her, we sang a different note on the end. She tried again, but we did the same thing. We wanted to sing our own notes. As our leader, Astrid didn't know what was going on, but in the end, she said with a laugh, "OK, whatever. You guys just do what you want there."

As a leader, sometimes you want to control every single note. You have a clear direction and steps on how to get there. You feel as if your way is the "right" way or the "only" way. However, there are times when you have to surrender control. **You must allow your people to sing their own notes loudly and proudly.**

Seth Godin, in his book *Tribes*, said, "The art of leadership is understanding what you can't compromise on." And, of course, this means you also must know what things you *can* compromise on – the things that won't impact the quality of the result.

If you allow your people to sing their own notes sometimes, you'll get their buy in and trust. They'll feel empowered and take ownership. You have to let go of being right. If you control every single note, they'll feel frustrated, as though they don't have a voice at all. They'll think it's your song, not theirs.

How do you conduct your pub choir?

Do your people sing in harmony?

Are you creating something magical together?

Do you allow your people to sing their own notes?

SEEK TO UNDERSTAND

A superhero likes things to be logical and rational, with a clear cause and effect. They want to feel in control and be able to predict the outcome of any situation. However, when it comes to leading people, things can be anything but predictable!

A certain approach may work for one person but not another, or maybe not even with the same person in a different situation. This can be frustrating and leave you second guessing your effectiveness as a leader.

You must always remember that people do things for their reasons, not yours.

When I think about my children, my flesh and blood, I birthed them, nurtured them, spend every day of my life interacting with them, yet they still see the world differently to me. Sometimes, I sit at the dinner table with my three and think to myself, "Who are you people and where did you come from?"

Now, think about what happens in the workplace. As a leader, you're trying to influence people who you've perhaps just met. You probably know little about their background, upbringing and values, but you expect them to see the world as you do. They don't, and this is a great thing. Diversity of viewpoints brings about innovation and creativity. It's difficult to know what your people think, let alone lift their performance, unless you take the time to listen to them. A great leader listens and genuinely tries to understand others' points of view.

A super coach has an abundance of **curiosity**.

Curiosity is a fundamental ingredient of great leadership. As a super coach, you need a hungry mind and willingness to learn. This is more important now than ever because we work in a fast-paced, innovative and uncertain business environment.

When asked recently to name the number-one attribute CEOs will need to succeed in the turbulent times ahead, Michael Dell, chief executive of Dell Technologies, replied: "I would place my bet on curiosity." Dell was responding to a 2015 PwC survey of more than 1,000 CEOs, many of whom cited curiosity and open mindedness as the traits that are becoming increasingly critical to great leadership in challenging times.[18]

Curiosity results in two things:

---

18 Berger, W. "Why Curious People Are Destined for the C-Suite", Harvard Business Review, 11 September, 2015. https://hbr.org/2015/09/why-curious-people-are-destined-for-the-c-suite

1. You will be less judgmental and more accepting of diverse opinions. You will seek to understand, and your people will feel valued and listened to.
2. You will be able to accept ambiguity and uncertainty. You will be energised by the complexity of a leadership situation rather than intimidated by it. You will handle being uncomfortable, experiment more and take risks.

It's a bit like doing a big jigsaw puzzle. At the start, there are pieces everywhere. It's all over the place. You have a few bits over here that go together, and a few bits over there that look similar. You might get all the corner pieces in place. The most important thing is to stay with the uncertainty. Don't let the fact you don't know how everything fits together discourage you. Over time, by staying with your curiosity, the puzzle starts coming together. You say, "Oh, I see now. These pieces belong over here, and that blue section is actually the sea, not the sky. I've got it." There is a new and deeper level of understanding. The process gets faster, and you finish the puzzle and achieve the result.

Leading with curiosity is like that. Sometimes, one piece of the puzzle or situation doesn't make sense in isolation. You need to find out more. You have to ask more questions. You must discover the context of the situation, learn more, and be OK with the uncertainty. Once you gain a greater understanding, you can move into action and start making effective, well-informed decisions.

If you lack curiosity as a leader, you'll become stagnant and conservative. You won't listen to others, take risks or push boundaries. You'll rush decisions in your need for certainty and closure, instead of seeking new ideas and different opinions from your people. You'll do everything you can to validate your own opinion in your need to be "right", alienating your people and losing their trust.

One of the greatest needs we have as human beings is to feel understood, that someone "gets us". Our children want to be able to share their ideas, feelings and opinions without fear of being judged. They want you to accept them for who they are. And guess what? So do the people in your team.

When you consider the rapid changes occurring in our workplaces, it's not hard to understand why your people might feel anxious and uncertain in their roles. As their leader, it's your job to listen to them and provide certainty, confidence and direction. Empower them to speak up and share their ideas and feelings.

Once your people feel understood, once you have listened to them without judgement or agenda, they will be open to listening to you. They'll feel valued and want to make their unique contribution to the success of your team. They'll trust you and be loyal to you. It's only from this position of mutual understanding that you can genuinely inspire, engage and motivate your people.

So, what gets in the way of effective listening?

You have so much going on operationally in your role that you may feel you don't have the time to listen. Sometimes in a new leadership position, you want to impress and get "runs on the board"; you want to bring about change and get noticed. Maybe this is driven by the fear that if you don't prove yourself quickly, "they" are not going to think you're up to the job. This fear drives your behaviour as you try to prove your worth, and you forget to take the time to truly listen to your team.

"Oh, I'm sorry. Did the middle of my sentence interrupt the beginning of yours?"

Slow your pace and take the time to understand what's going on for your people. Ask what they need from you to perform at their best. Doing this takes courage and strength of character. You need to listen to gain a deep understanding of your people's issues.

You see, from deep understanding comes influence. Influence doesn't come from a title or position; it comes from understanding your team as a whole, and each team member individually. It's the same with any relationship. Good luck trying to influence a teenage son if he doesn't feel understood. You might get lip service – in other words, compliance – but you'll never get commitment.

Ideas for effective listening:

- **Check your mindset and intention**

  Do you want to understand the other person or merely get your point of view across? Remember, it's their story, not yours. Keep an open mind. Stay curious, and leave your assumptions and biases to one side. As soon as you start judging, you compromise your effectiveness as a listener and leader.

- **Give your full attention**

  Make sure you face the person and maintain eye contact. In most Western cultures, eye contact is considered a basic element of effective communication. A lawyer once told me that when she was typing away on her computer and one of her team members came into her office, she had a simple ritual: stop, turn and smile. I like this. Remember to set aside papers, books, your phone and other distractions. Make the person feel valued.

- **Be aware of non-verbal cues**

  A person's body language and facial expressions can give you a real insight into their true feelings, sometimes even more so than their words. Watch for any incongruence between what they say and what their body tells you.

- **Practise empathy**

  When listening to someone talk about a problem, refrain from suggesting solutions. If they want your advice, they'll ask for it. Show you understand where the speaker is coming from by reflecting the speaker's feelings. "You must be excited by the new project," or, "I can see that you're feeling confused." If the speaker's feelings are hidden or unclear, occasionally paraphrase the content of their message back to them. Sometimes, a simple nod shows your understanding. The idea is to give the other person proof you're actively listening.

- **Allow silence**

  Most of us feel awkward when there's silence. Don't be tempted to fill it with your words. If you allow the silence just to be, the other person will continue to open up. Some people need time and space to gather their thoughts, especially if they're talking about an emotional issue.

- **Ask for clarification**

  Of course, when you don't understand something, you should ask the other person to explain it to you. Rather than interrupt, wait until they pause, then say something like, "I didn't understand what you just said about…"

Super coaches are great listeners. If you work on your listening skills, you are destined to be a better, more compassionate leader.

"Listen, or your tongue will make you deaf."

- NATIVE AMERICAN PROVERB

ASK FOR HELP

I remember last year being worried about a family situation. The kind of worry that keeps you up at night and wakes you in the early hours of the morning. It leaves you with that awful feeling in the pit of your stomach. I'm sure you've experienced it yourself.

Finally, late one Friday night, I decided to pick up the phone and ask a friend for help. It took some back-and-forth text messages and a good dose of courage, but I did it.

You see, sometimes we can be reluctant to ask for help. We can be embarrassed and feel like a failure. If you're like me, you have this image of yourself as a strong, independent and capable leader, but just because you're all those things doesn't mean you don't need others, nor does it mean you should feel any less for putting up your hand and admitting you need help. You know what they say about a problem shared?

It's like having the flare gun in your boat as a safety precaution. The flare gun is there for a reason. You shouldn't wait until the boat is sinking and your head is just above the water to discharge the flare. By then, it's too late – you're going under.

The superhero leader feels like they can't ask for help. They have to appear powerful and invincible at all times; it comes with the role. It's up to them to save the day, with full responsibility on their shoulders.

However, the super coach knows that sometimes, everyone needs a little help.

Does it feel scary to ask for help? Yes.

Does it feel vulnerable? You bet.

But if you continue to struggle with an issue and keep it inside, it will just get bigger. It will consume you.

As a leader, there will be many moments when you're not sure what you're doing, and it feels like you're stumbling in the dark. The secret is to know who to send up the flare to, and when.

The fear of being vulnerable and labelled as "soft" or "weak" can hold you back. You worry people will think less of you, that you're not coping in your role. You believe it will negatively impact your reputation and leadership brand. However, US researcher and writer Brené Brown says the number-one trust-earning behaviour at work is asking for help. So, it's time to let go of our judgement about reaching out to others and admit that we need their support.

Brown says, "Until we can receive with an open heart, we're never really giving with an open heart. When we attach judgement to receiving help, we knowingly or unknowingly attach judgement to giving help."

That Friday night, I received help from my friend with an open heart, knowing that in the future, it will be my turn to support someone else.

You see, when you ask for help, it:

- Humanises you as a leader. You're real and authentic.
- Allows others to feel safe to ask for help. You set the unwritten ground rules as the leader. If you can do it, so can everyone else.
- Creates a collaborative, rather than competitive, culture, where egos are left at the door. No one knows everything (not even the boss), and we all need help sometimes.
- Allows you to learn and grow from others. You get to ask more questions, receive advice, and see your problem from a different perspective.
- Builds high-trust relationships.

There will be times when you ask yourself what the hell you're doing. You can read every leadership theory, but it's not until you're in charge of a group of people that you fully appreciate what the role involves, and you start to wonder, "Why did I take this promotion?" You question your decisions, self-doubt creeps in, and you feel out of your comfort zone.

In leadership, you need to embrace the unknown territory. Acknowledge that you will make mistakes because, guess what? That's perfectly OK. You won't be the first leader to stuff things up. We all make mistakes, but it's how you handle them that influences your team.

Often when we fail or make a mistake, we react immediately, blaming others or making excuses. We might even try to hide it and hope no one finds out. These reactions can be a default response when you feel under threat and things are out of control. They're a way to protect yourself.

But, ultimately, they destroy trust in your relationships, and no one will follow a leader they don't trust.

So, what do you do when you make a mistake?

- **Create space.** Create some space between the mistake and your response if you can. Don't react immediately because you may revert to blame or avoidance.
- **Self-reflect.** Take a good look in the mirror and ask yourself, "What happened? What did I learn from this?" Diagnose the problem. You may need the help of a trusted colleague to fully appreciate what happened. We all have blind spots as leaders.
- **Accept responsibility.** Step up and take accountability. Be the first to break the news – don't hide it. Own the mistake, even if you didn't directly cause it. Don't minimise the problem – be vulnerable and apologise.
- **Take action.** Take the necessary steps to eliminate the risk of the same mistake happening again. Fix the initial problem, then dig a little deeper to see whether there is an issue with a more extensive process.

By owning your mistakes and asking for help, your team will see you as a leader they can rely on and trust. We all need a time out sometimes; things can get too much, and you need to take a step back. That's OK. This is the time to empower your people to step up and take some responsibility. Share the load. What an opportunity to see what your people are capable of! Let them grow and learn.

Geese flying formation

Have you ever noticed a flock of geese flying in a V formation? As each bird flaps its wings, it creates an uplift for the bird immediately following. By flying in V formation, the flock adds at least 71% greater flying range than if each bird flew on its own.[19]

When a goose falls out of formation, it suddenly feels the drag and resistance of trying to go it alone, and quickly gets back into formation to take advantage of the lifting power of the bird in front. When the head goose tires, it rotates back in the wing, and another goose flies the point.

I think we can learn a lot about leadership from the goose formation. You don't have to do it alone. Your team is there to support you, and together, you can share the load and play to your strengths. It makes sense to take turns taking the lead. After all, the head goose gets tired!

Don't be frighted to ask for help. You show your true leadership character during the tough times, so put the denial and excuses aside and be vulnerable. Your people will respect and admire you for it. Let others take the lead and empower them to step up.

---

19 Lissaman, P.B.S. & Shollenberger, C.A. (1970). *Formation flight of birds.* Science 168(3934): 1003–1005 https://science.sciencemag.org/content/168/3934/1003

ENGAGE IN CONVERSATIONS THAT MATTER

Conversations build relationships. As a leader, do you have conversations that matter? Conversations that build confidence and awareness, inspire action, spark creativity and develop trust?

As a super coach, you need to promote open and direct feedback. Problems arise when leaders are unsure of how to structure their feedback or start the conversation. If you don't put the time and effort into giving effective feedback and having coaching conversations, it can demotivate your team members.

Feedback should be a gift of information. It's a means of letting your people know what they are doing well and how they can become more effective. When feedback is about improving performance, it creates strong relationships.

So, how can you give effective feedback?

- You must first be open to receiving feedback. If you can't handle receiving feedback, how can others accept it from you? In the words of Brené Brown, "If you're not in the arena getting your ass kicked, then I'm not interested in your feedback."
- Give feedback based on first-hand knowledge when possible. Structuring feedback on what you have observed directly, rather than on what someone else has told you, will make the conversation easier.
- Even if the feedback is negative, approach the conversation as a positive opportunity to remind your team member of your expectations and gain commitment from them.
- Be specific and give examples. Feedback such as, "You're doing a great job," is too general and doesn't provide your team member with any details. What exactly do you want them to continue doing? What is contributing to the "great job"?
- Avoid using "but" or "however", as these words undermine your key message. No feedback sandwiches, either – this is where you say a positive comment, then a negative one, then finish on a positive note. People will only take away what they want to hear and ignore the rest.
- Be future oriented. Describe what would make a difference in the future, not just what went wrong.

Your people will be more willing to accept feedback if you are fair and consistent. Above all, you must show them respect.

Teams want to know they are valued and that what they think matters. They want to feel heard. This is when a healthy dose of curiosity is needed (as we discussed earlier in "Seek to Understand"). You must leave your assumptions and prejudices at the door during your feedback conversations.

A question I always find helpful in any feedback and coaching situation is, "What do I know for sure?" It's also the title of one of my favourite books by Oprah Winfrey.

I remember facilitating a workshop early in my career and noticing one woman in the group. She made no eye contact with me the entire day. She didn't crack a smile, not even at my funniest of stories (and I'm pretty funny!), and she hardly wrote a thing in her workbook. She ignored my instructions and spent most of the day doodling and daydreaming.

I couldn't believe it. What had I done wrong? She obviously didn't like me or what I had to say. She wasn't interested in any of the content and thought it was a complete waste of time. I drove home from that workshop feeling frustrated, deflated and disheartened.

The next week, as part of the course, I had scheduled one-on-one debriefing sessions with each participant. As you can imagine, I was dreading the phone conversation with her. However, the funniest thing happened when I made the call. Before I could say anything, she apologised. She told me about an argument she'd had with her long-term partner the weekend before the workshop, and she had been questioning whether they had a future together. She said her head wasn't in the right place that day and, in hindsight, she probably shouldn't have come.

The lesson I learnt from that experience was always to ask myself, "What do I know for sure?"

In this situation, I had quickly climbed the Ladder of Inference. The Ladder of Inference is a model that explains how you can move from one piece of data (a comment or observation) through a series of mental processes to a conclusion.[20]

THE LADDER OF INFERENCE

In my example, I selected observable data from the participant – no eye contact, no smiling and no writing in her workbook. I quickly added meaning to the data – she's disengaged and not interested. Then I drew a conclusion – she doesn't like me or anything I have to say. Was my conclusion correct? Not at all. When I coach clients, I often find the same flawed reasoning in their conclusions.

We can see or make up issues all around us, and, of course, sometimes they're correct, but more often than not, there is something else going on we're unaware of. We don't see things as they are; we see them as *we* are. The Ladder of Inference can be dangerous because we can climb it extremely quickly. You

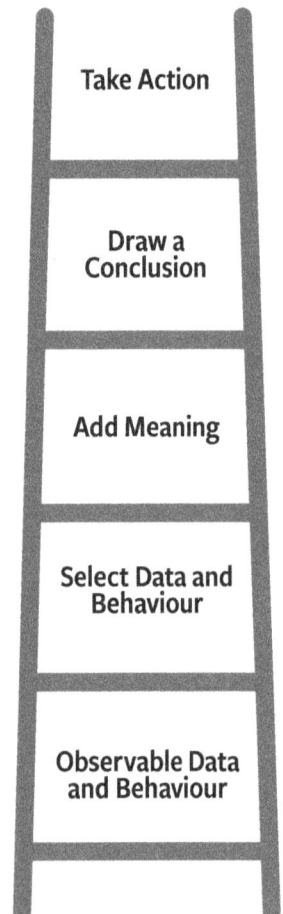

Take Action

Draw a Conclusion

Add Meaning

Select Data and Behaviour

Observable Data and Behaviour

20 The Ladder of Inference", Mind Tools. https://www.mindtools.com/pages/article/newTMC_91.htm

can be oblivious to the fact you're only selecting some of the observable data. This means you act and give feedback based on only part of the story. Nobody else sees your thought processes or knows what stages you have gone through to reach your conclusions. All they see is the action you take, and this can undermine your effectiveness as a leader.

How can you stop yourself from climbing the Ladder of Inference?

1. Firstly, accept that you will always draw meaning and inferences from what others say and do. It's natural.
2. The key is to be aware of this process and test your assumptions instead of blindly accepting them.
3. Ask your people more questions about what they are thinking. Practise empathic listening and seek first to understand.
4. The quickest way to go back down the ladder and challenge your conclusions is to ask that simple question: What do I know for sure?

See every conversation as a coaching opportunity. Remember, coaching is about looking forward. Your feedback should move your people from where they are now to where they want to be and help them put the steps in place to achieve it.

As a leader, you need to ask the right questions to empower action and expand your people's thinking. The right questions can change a person's long-standing beliefs. It can shift their mood or reveal a possibility they had never considered before. Ask open-ended questions when you want to stimulate creative thinking. Ask closed questions when you seek commitment from a team member, particularly at the end of a coaching conversation when actions have been agreed upon.

A helpful model for coaching conversations is the GROW (goal, reality, options, way forward) model. This model was developed in the 1980s by business coaches Graham Alexander, Alan Fine and Sir John Whitmore.[21] I have used this framework for many years with my coaching clients, and it works. It's a simple yet powerful four-step process that will keep the feedback conversation on track.

By using the GROW model to structure your feedback, you will enhance your team's performance and create awareness and commitment. Your coaching conversations will boost the confidence of your people, increase accountability and, ultimately, help you achieve your goals.

As a super coach, you want to create a culture of feedback. Get out there and share your feedback with your team members, and be open to receiving it yourself. This is the only way we all learn, feel empowered and get better at what we do.

G - GOAL	What is the goal of the conversation? State the objective clearly at the start. It may simply be to make the person aware of their behaviour and its impact, or similar.
R - REALITY	Explore the current situation, and listen empathetically. Acknowledge what you hear. Ask questions to help others open up, e.g. What's missing? What's working? What are the obstacles?
O - OPTIONS	What options can team members think of that will create progress? Explore alternatives. Encourage creative brainstorming and listen to ideas.
W - WAY FORWARD	Help team members develop action plans by identifying resources needed, who is involved, timeframes, obstacles and solutions.

---

21 "The GROW Model of Coaching and Mentoring", Mind Tools. https://www.mindtools.com/pages/article/newLDR_89.htm

GIVE UP
CONTROL

Recently, my eldest son, Tommy, got his learner's licence. He passed the online test on a Wednesday night, and then on Thursday (his 16th birthday), I picked him up from school at lunchtime and he collected his licence from the Department of Transport. He was behind the steering wheel by 1 o'clock. And it was the most terrifying experience of my life!

I so wanted to be that cool and calm parent, encouraging and supportive, but instead I spent the whole time in a state of panic, saying, "Brake... brake... BRAKE!!!" I knew this wasn't the way to lead, teach or mentor, but I just couldn't help myself.

I've been thinking about why this experience was so scary for me. I think it came down to two things. Firstly, I felt a huge loss of control, and secondly, I perceived there was a high risk involved.

The minute I moved into the passenger seat, I lost control and didn't like it. I've been a lawyer for a long time, and I've interviewed my fair share of clients who have been seriously injured in motor vehicle accidents. I've seen how they can devastate lives, so to me, driving is a high-risk activity. As the passenger, I was completely out of my comfort zone.

Now, this was not the first time I'd felt like this. There have been moments in my career when I've been reluctant to hand over control. Because being in control feels good, right? It feels powerful, like being a superhero.

As a leader, it's understandable that you want to keep your hands firmly on the wheel at all times. It can be tough to hand your keys to someone else. This is particularly the case when there is a high risk involved – maybe a project with your most important client, or a big sales pitch.

I recently spoke to a client, a co-owner of a professional services firm. He discussed with me his role in the firm and his strong personal connection with his clients. He attended all the sales meetings with these clients. However, he faced a dilemma. The business was growing, with plans to expand interstate, and it wasn't going to be possible for him to do all this work himself. It was time for him to give up some control and provide an opportunity for someone in the firm to step up.

In leadership (just like in parenthood), sometimes you need to relinquish control. Terrifying? Yes, but absolutely necessary if you want to grow the skills and experience of your people.

So, how can you do this successfully? How can you sit in the passenger seat without being in a constant state of panic?

- Firstly, you need to have confidence in the person you're handing over control to. You must hold a certain level of trust in their capability. This is why it's so important to start developing your people's leadership skills from the start of their career. There's no point waiting until someone is appointed in a formal leadership position, and then starting their training and mentoring. I hear so often from companies that there are not enough "ready now" leaders.
- Secondly, you can employ the "dual control" technique. This is just like being in a driving instructor's car, where the instructor has a brake and accelerator on their side. What is your leadership succession plan? Who are the up-and-coming leaders in your organisation? Start handing the keys to them now so they can drive around the block with you by their side. You've got the brake right there if you need it. Take them to that big client meeting, let them present to the board, allow them to facilitate a segment at the next strategy day.

RISK AND CONTROL

High risk – SUPERVISE (✓)

It's your role to supervise and support your people through a high-risk situation – something they haven't done before or a project with a major client. This is the time to engage the dual control technique discussed above. Let them explore and learn but support them along the way. If you fail to provide sufficient supervision and control during this time, your people will feel like they're drowning. They'll lose confidence and never want to step out of their comfort zone again. They may feel let down by you, and it erodes their trust in your leadership.

Low risk – STRETCH (✓)

On the other hand, when there is little to low risk involved in a situation, it's time for you to take a step back and allow your people to be independent. Now is the time to stretch them a little and see what they're capable of. Give them enough stretch so they can grow and learn in a safe environment. You need to loosen your grip, stop micromanaging, and relinquish control, giving them the opportunity to grow and learn.

"The person most in control is the person who can give up control."

- FREDERICK SALOMON PERLS

DISCOVER
THEIR TALENT

A s a leader, you're also busy. Let's face it, every hour is rush hour for a leader! The pace is go, go, go. And the higher you climb the corporate ladder, the faster the pace. You sprint to catch that next train, oblivious to anyone or anything around you.

Often, you don't make getting to know the people who are new to your organisation a priority. You're too busy. At the other end of the spectrum, you may ignore long-standing employees, assuming you already know them and their strengths.

In 2007, a social experiment was conducted in the metro train station in Washington, DC. A musician played the violin for about 45 minutes, and during that time, thousands of people entered the metro. However, only a handful stopped to listen. About 20 people gave the musician money but continued to walk at their usual pace. When he finished playing, no one noticed, and there was no applause or recognition.

No one knew this, but the violinist was Joshua Bell, an acclaimed classical violinist and one of the most celebrated musicians in the world. He had played one of the most intricate pieces of music ever written on a violin worth $3.5 million. Days earlier, people had paid to see Bell perform at Boston's Symphony Hall – it was a packed audience.

But at the metro, people were too busy, distracted, and rushed to appreciate the incredible talent right there in front of them.

We can be quick to judge people and pigeonhole them, which means we fail to notice their growth and development, their new capabilities. All of us are continually learning, and we need new experiences and challenges to keep us stimulated and engaged.

One of your key responsibilities as a super coach is to identify the talents of your people and nurture and reward these talents. You play a critical role in facilitating their learning. Make it easy for them to grow their self-awareness, knowledge and expertise. If you can focus on the development of your people, you will build a team that is engaged, committed and performing at its best.

A CEO I once worked with told me he believed his job was to find out what people were good at and let them do it. I love this!

So, how can you identify and nurture the talents of your people?

- **Slow down.** I know you want to make that next train but slow the pace. Agility and speed are great when it comes to processes – when you need to fail at things quickly to find out what works best – but when it comes to your people, slow is fast. If you rush, you will miss out on discovering and leveraging the talent you have in front of you.

- **Be inquisitive.** Find out more about the people who work with you – their values, purpose and strengths. What are their goals? What turns them on? What do they want to learn next? Then, ask questions that will challenge them. Get your people to see their problems and obstacles in a different light and open their minds to what else is possible. No one learns much from being told what to do.

- **Create connection.** As a super coach, it's your role to connect your people with the vision and purpose of your organisation. Get them to understand why they do what they do, how they contribute to the firm's purpose, and what they can learn to increase their influence and impact.

- **Create the right learning environment.** You want your people to be in flow; to have just the right amount of stretch and challenge to experiment, grow and learn. Too much stretch and they'll feel anxious, stressed and burnt out. Too little and they'll lose their mojo and disengage. Your people must be intrinsically motivated to learn. You need to create a culture of learning in your team that encourages and rewards those who seek personal and professional growth. Each team member will learn differently: some will want to read; others will want to do. Some will want formal learning, such as the opportunity to do further study at university, while others will prefer a more informal approach.

Once you have discovered the talents of your people, it's time to give them meaningful work that allows them to use these talents to their full potential. Let them shine! Take a step back and get out of their way. Let them find their own solutions and methods, and, of course, let them fail (tough, I know). You must empower your people to make their own decisions.

When each team member plays to their strengths, you are stronger as a team. It's vital that everyone understands each other's roles and responsibilities, and that each role is equally valued and celebrated.

"A team is not a bunch of people with job titles, but a congregation of individuals, each of whom has a role that is understood by other members."

– MEREDITH BELBIN

TALENT REWARD AND CELEBRATION

A super coach knows the impact that reward and recognition have on their team members. It's huge!

I remember one morning coming into the office, and there on my desk was a white envelope with my name written on the front. Inside was a handwritten card from the CEO, thanking me for the enthusiasm and positivity I brought to the firm. I kept that card on my desk for years.

It's your job to show your people their value and to shine a spotlight on their talents. Never underestimate the power of your acknowledgement and gratitude. It's your job to believe in your people before they believe in themselves.

Tell your people how proud you are of them and what you value most about their contribution. Take the time to celebrate their successes and share them with the rest of the organisation.

Questions to discover more about your people:

- What are the talents of each of your team members?
- Do your people find meaning and purpose in their work?
- Do they understand the "why" behind their work duties?
- What motivates each team member?
- What do they want to learn next?
- When was the last time you made it possible for your team to be proud of their work?
- What are you doing to make work rewarding and inspiring for your people?
- What does a great day look like for each of your team members?

"Talent can't be taught, but it can be awakened."

– WALLACE STEGNER

DON'T FORGET YOUR MIDDLE CHILDREN

As a leader, you typically have three groups of people within your team. Your most senior team members have been with you for a while now. They're experienced, perhaps leading their own teams. They've found their place in your organisation, are well-known, have built a strong reputation, and are happy doing their "thing". Their achievements have been rewarded and recognised. They're respected and trusted and, as such, have a high degree of autonomy and flexibility. They feel empowered to make decisions and take responsibility.

You also have your recent recruits – your newbies who have just joined your team, all bright and shiny. They're enthusiastic, optimistic and eager to learn. They're discovering a new role and finding their feet in your organisation. They tend to have less responsibility as they go through the onboarding process, but everything is exciting and new for them, and you welcome them warmly. Their induction reminds them why this organisation is the place for them. They hear success stories; it seems there is endless opportunity and potential. They also feel empowered to explore their new surroundings and test the boundaries.

And then you have your "middle children" – team members who have been in your organisation for a year or more, but are not yet part of the furniture. For these people, the honeymoon phase is over. That new-job feel has well and truly worn off. Their initial optimism and excitement have dissipated, and reality has well and truly set in. They often work long hours, deal with client demands daily, and it's hard work. They feel neglected and overlooked.

As a leader, you're juggling priorities and feel run off your feet. When you're busy, your middle children are often the first to be forgotten.

It's easy to connect with your senior team members. You probably attend meetings with them, ask them for a second opinion, and attend functions together. Similarly, with your new recruits, there are meet-and-greet events to attend, as well as onboarding and induction training to deliver. There are lots of touchpoints for your senior and new team members, but not so many for your middle children.

Research from Friday, a company that tracks employee happiness, and staffing firm Robert Half found that, typically, employees are their happiest and least stressed during their first year in a new job. The study found that happiness levels drop and stress levels increase significantly in their second year. Those levels rebound in the following years.[22]

Similarly, in the legal profession, data from the Legal Firm of Choice Survey 2019 found that on a scale of one to five, lawyers with less than one year of experience have a satisfaction rating of 3.91, which drops to 3.41 a few years later. "When graduate lawyers enter law firms, their satisfaction levels are relatively high, but this drops off significantly once lawyers have one to three years of experience under their belts," says Momentum Intelligence head of research Michael Johnson.[23] I'm sure this is the case for other industries, as well.

As a leader, if you neglect these critical people in your team, you risk them walking out the door to find the next new, shiny opportunity – a new workplace where they will be appreciated and valued. Think about this – all that time, money and energy spent recruiting, onboarding, training, culturally immersing them and building relationships, only to have these people leave your team for another opportunity.

Your middle children need to feel valued. They need to know their place and be empowered in their role.

So, how do you keep your middle children engaged, excited and productive?

---

[22] Brooks, C. "Be Happy: How to Extend the Honeymoon Phase of a New Job", Business News Daily, 21 February, 2019. https://www.businessnews-daily.com/9741-employee-job-honeymoon-phase.html

[23] Doraisamy, J. "2 in 5 young lawyers intend to walk out the door", Lawyers Weekly, 4 September 2019. https://www.lawyersweekly.com.au/biglaw/26431-2-in-5-young-lawyers-intend-to-walk-out-the-door

- **Create a peer squad.** Work friends can make their days more fun. To deepen these connections, make a concerted effort to promote social and professional events to build camaraderie.

- **Promote proactivity.** Build a culture where your people are proactive and talk to you about taking on assignments, instead of waiting for you to assign them new projects.

- **Show appreciation.** Reward and recognise your middle children's hard work and dedication. Take the time to give positive feedback and make sure they know their efforts are noticed.

- **Dive deeper.** Get to know them on a deeper level and find out more about who they are, their values, and their purpose.

- **Set goals together.** Find out what your middle children want to learn next, the skills and knowledge they want to develop, and help them achieve it by setting a plan of action.

I remember when I was a middle child working for a company. There were times when I felt invisible and unappreciated. It felt like one of the senior leaders would have to retire or die before I would get a promotion. (A little extreme, I know!) I had big ambitions, but it was tough to stay motivated and engaged year after year. Then, a couple of leaders in the firm invested in my learning and development to keep me on track and working hard.

Your middle children are such an asset to your team. If treated well, they will lift the morale of your entire team, be brand ambassadors for your organisation, and go above and beyond for your clients.

KNOW WHEN
TO HOLD 'EM

G aining the love and respect of my friends is important to me. I thought I did this by supporting them, showing compassion and a willingness to help, and being there when they needed me, but last year, I found out what really gains people's respect!

It was my friend's 50th birthday party. We were sharing a beautiful grazing table and pouring drinks from the frozen margarita machine – a great night! A bit later in the evening, one of my favourite songs – Kenny Rogers' "The Gambler" (no judgement, please!) – came on. I shot up and belted out the song from start to finish, word for word – possibly helped by the margarita slushies. When I finished singing, there was an explosion of applause. Well, that's how I remember it, anyway…

A few weeks later, when I caught up with these friends again, they said, "We always liked you, Midja, but it wasn't until we heard you singing 'The Gambler' that you gained our full respect." If only I had known it was that easy!

I love the song "The Gambler" for two reasons. The first is that it reminds me of sitting with my dad on a Saturday afternoon, singing that song on our front verandah. When I hear it, I think of him.

Secondly, I love the song because it contains advice I give to my clients all the time:

"You've got to know when to hold 'em,

Know when to fold 'em,

Know when to walk away and know when to run."

As a super coach, you need to be bold and decisive. You need to take action and not be afraid to take risks. But sometimes, you need to show patience and restraint. You need to listen and understand.

There are many times when you will have to confidently take your seat at the card table, play your hand, and show your cards. But other times, you must hold your cards close. You need to know when to keep your opinion, point of view and advice to yourself.

And then there will be times when you'll have to fold and let an issue go. Remember, you will be dealt another hand in the future. You simply need to wait for a better situation, a better time.

I believe there are three leadership situations when it's best to hold 'em:

1. **When you are highly emotional around an issue**

    If you can't keep a poker face, don't play. Now, I love passion and excitement, but as a leader, you need to recognise the distinction between being passionate and being impulsive and reckless. In these situations, it might be better for another person to handle the situation, or to wait until that highly emotional state is over.

2. **When you encounter an unexpected or unusual response to an issue**

    This is when someone else's behaviour is uncharacteristic, even off the chart. You're not sure why they're acting this way, and you may never know. This is not the time to show your hand or push, because pushing will do more harm than good. Give the person space. I've observed that when you give people space, they often come back and acknowledge their over-the-top reaction.

3. **When you're in a new leadership role**

    This can be the time when you want to rush to the leadership table and show your cards, all your aces. You want to make a big contribution. But, just like a gambler, you need to observe the table first. See what cards have already fallen and the reactions to those cards. You need to get to know the dealer and the other players. There is not enough trust or confidence to play just yet. You need time to gather more information and read the state of play.

Being a super coach is a beautiful balancing act of showing confidence and humility to build trust. You want to be authentic and vulnerable, but this doesn't mean that every day, in every situation, you play an open hand. If you can learn to know when to show 'em, when to hold 'em, and when to fold 'em, you'll gain considerable influence and get that balancing act just right.

GET THEM
THROUGH THE
BORING, BORING,
BORING

I've been sitting at this table, writing and editing this book for a while. My three kids have been at home during this time due to COVID-19. They're home schooling and looking to me as a source of entertainment. But with a book-writing deadline, I don't have much time to spare.

My 15-year-old daughter, Sophie, said to me last week, "Mum, you're just sooo boring!"

Ouch!

Many years ago, I was at our annual Christmas party: five families who met when all our boys were in kindy together and stayed close friends ever since. Every year, we get together the week before Christmas for a feast and a few bottles of champagne. There is always a Secret Santa gift-giving ceremony.

This particular year, a friend's daughter was super excited about her present. She was four or five years old. Her name was called, and she ran up to grab her gift. She ripped the paper and inside was a little baking set, which I thought was very cute, but she was less impressed with the present. She threw it down and yelled, "BORING, BORING, BORING!"

We all burst out laughing. It was just the funniest thing to watch, but I'm not so sure my friend Rachel, who gave the present, could see the funny side. Lol.

For all of us, some parts of our job are just BORING, BORING, BORING! We find them tedious and unmotivating.

For me, editing a book, getting chapter sequences right, and checking grammar and references are not fun. They're not tasks I enjoy doing, but I know they're important to do if I want to be a keynote speaker.

So, how do I stay motivated?

It's easy. By having a **clear vision**.

As I write this book, in my mind, I have a vision of holding the book in my hands, reading from it at the launch (with a glass of champagne in my hand!), being up on stage, taking off the cape and mask, and delivering a keynote. The vision is so real to me that I can *feel* it. It's like I'm already there.

As a super coach, you must do the same thing for your people. You need to give them a clear vision.

Parts of your people's role will annoy and frustrate them. They will dislike doing some things, but these tasks are essential to their role. No job is all unicorns, butterflies and rainbows all the time. Work can be tough and demanding.

You need to motivate your team to get through these time toughs by encouraging them to imagine the outcome. Why do they do what they do? Make it vivid – like they can touch it, smell it, feel it. Keep reminding them of this. Hook them in!

A super coach harnesses the power of **anticipation**.

Social psychologists Liz Dunn and Mike Norton describe anticipation as "free happiness". As an article in *Psychology Today* says, "It costs no extra to harness the power of anticipation, and yet it can add so much more excitement to an already-good experience."[24]

The brain chemical dopamine is released when we anticipate something. Dopamine is future oriented, motivating us to do great things. As a leader, you can build anticipation and suspense for your people, and throw in a good dose of the unexpected to create a feel-good dopamine hit.

A mentor once told me you only need two things in life to be happy:

1. Someone to love; and
2. Something to look forward to

---

[24] Kurtz, J.L. "Harnessing the Power of Anticipation", *Psychology Today*, 2 May 2017. https://www.psychologytoday.com/au/blog/happy-trails/201705/harnessing-the-power-anticipation

So, what are you doing to give your people something to look forward to? How, as a leader, can you harness the power of anticipation in your workplace?

The most powerful action you can take is to embed rituals – daily, weekly, monthly, and yearly – to create not only a sense of rhythm in your team, but also a sense of anticipation. These rituals can be big or small and may involve some form of reward. The most important thing is to make them connected to your people's work, their behaviours, your organisation's values and culture, and the achievement of meaningful goals.

When your people have a healthy sense of anticipation, they will:

- Be committed and engaged
- Be motivated to go above and beyond
- Have high energy, optimism and a can-do attitude
- Get through the tough and stressful moments
- Have the persistence to keep moving forward

If you want your people to achieve a goal, they must anticipate the outcome of achieving it. What will be the result? What will it feel like?

If your people don't have anything to look forward to in the workplace, they'll become disengaged and stagnant. They won't go above and beyond; they'll procrastinate and give up when the going gets tough. There'll be no buzz, no positive energy, and no serious commitment. People will ring in for that sick day, give you pushback, and only look forward to 5 o'clock on a Friday afternoon.

As a super coach, you can engage and empower your people to get through the hard times by speaking to their imagination and hearts.

In his book, *Mastering the Rockefeller Habits*, Verne Harnish says:

"Visionaries intuitively understand what too many business executives have yet to learn, which is that it takes an idea or an image to anchor a message with its listening audience. To get people to storm the barricades on your behalf, you've got to give them a concept that connects not just with their heads, but their hearts."

You need to create a vision for your team members that appeals to all their senses, grabs their attention, and connects with their hearts. Your people will remember this, and commit to it.

FOR GOODNESS' SAKE, HAVE SOME FUN

Tell me, what's your favourite day of the working week?

Most people say Wednesday. Why? Because it's hump day, when they're on the downward slope to Friday afternoon when their "real" life begins. These same people feel sick to their stomachs on a Sunday afternoon, around 3pm, when they realise it's nearly time to go back to their dreaded workplace.

Is this how you want the people in your team to feel?

I think you'd agree that we all need some fun and laughter in our lives, and that shouldn't just happen between 5pm Friday and 8am Monday. Our work is supposed to be enjoyed.

"People rarely succeed unless they have fun in what they are doing."

– DALE CARNEGIE

A super coach takes their work seriously, but not themselves. They keep things light and fun in the office; they make time for play.

Play is so valuable because it:

- Stimulates the mind and imagination, increasing creativity
- Promotes problem solving and the ability to adapt to situations
- Is a great stress reliever and boosts happiness
- Increases productivity and focus
- Gives people permission to try new things and experiment, providing the space to fail safely
- Builds deep connections with others, boosting camaraderie and corporate empathy

So, my question for you is, do you make time to play every day? And what does your play look like?

Psychiatrist Stuart Brown, founder of the American National Institute for Play, says: "What all play has in common is that it offers a sense of engagement and pleasure, takes the player out of a sense of time and place, and the experience of doing it is more important than the outcome."[25]

---

[25] Wallace, J. "Play is important for adults, too", *The Sydney Morning Herald*, 22 May, 2017. https://www.smh.com.au/lifestyle/health-and-wellness/play-is-important-for-adults-too-20170522-gw9ysw.html

Brown says that although some people may appear more playful than others, we are all wired by evolution to play.

Sir Richard Branson is well-known for his playfulness in business. He says, "Try and keep bureaucracy to a minimum, and remind your team that business, as well as life, should be fun."

As leaders, it is our job to encourage play in the workplace, and become what I like to call "facilitators of fun"! It's time to put some play and humour back into our stressful days in the office. In fact, a survey conducted by Robert Half International showed that 91% of executives believed humour was imperative for career advancement, and 84% thought people with a sense of humour did better work.[26]

I've been lucky enough to be part of a learning and development team that liked to play and understood play's value. Throughout our learning experiences, we always incorporated playful activities, such as archery, morning walks, scavenger hunts, belly dancing, singing and even confetti cannons! All these activities were about engagement, pleasure and experiencing something different. It was about getting people out of their comfort zone from time to time and being a bit silly; letting the walls down and being vulnerable.

And who doesn't love a good laugh? When we laugh, it releases endorphins, making us feel good. Laughter is also contagious. If you see two people laughing at a joke you didn't hear, chances are that you will smile anyway – even if you don't realise it.

Perhaps the biggest benefit of laughter is the activation of both sides of the brain. Laughter kickstarts the limbic system, which

---

[26] "Is a sense of humour in the workplace good for your career?" Robert Half, 27 March, 2017. https://www.roberthalf.com.au/blog/jobseekers/sense-humour-workplace-good-your-career

connects the brain's right and left sides. This leads to greater learning opportunities and creativity.

Happier, livelier workplaces are full of energy and highly productive. Your people will enjoy coming to work; they'll feel part of a team and want to perform at their best.

As a super coach, model this behaviour. Be the first to have fun and encourage playfulness in your team.

A Final Note

You're a remarkable leader who wants to make a difference. I know that much. You want to lead a team of people who come to work each day to give their best. You want to see them succeed, learn and grow under your leadership. You want to empower them to think creatively and be responsible for their results.

I hope this book has given you some new insights, perspectives and actionable ideas on how to do just that!

Your people want a leader they can trust and admire; someone who makes them feel safe, valued and important. They want honesty, integrity and transparency. They also want to have some fun along the way, a good laugh, and to feel proud about the work they do.

When you become that leader, your people will remember you. You'll gain their loyalty and commitment and, as a result, achieve great things for your clients.

I want you to be a leader people want to follow. I want you to take off the cape and stop trying to be everything for everyone. Stop trying to be perfect.

I want you to stop hiding and instead show your people the real you. I want you to have the confidence and courage to be authentic and follow your passion; to be the super coach you're meant to be.

Quite simply, I want you to love leading!

Midja x

Work with Midja

As a renowned leadership expert, Midja facilitates corporate programs across Australia, as well as presenting at conferences and events, and conducting one-on-one mentoring.

There are a number of ways you can connect and work with Midja:

1. Book Midja to speak at your next conference or event.
2. Ask her to facilitate a leadership program in your organisation.
3. Join Midja's 'Women with Confidence' mentoring program.
4. Enrol in Midja's 'Ignite Your Leadership' online course.
5. Subscribe to Midja's weekly video blog 'Mondays with Midja'.
6. Follow, like and share Midja's updates online.

wwww.linkedin.com/in/midja

www.facebook.com/midja.leadership

www.instagram.com/midja_fisher/

www.midja.com.au
midja@midja.com.au
M: 0408 718 445

www.ingramcontent.com/pod-product-compliance
Lightning Source LLC
Chambersburg PA
CBHW030508210326
41597CB00013B/833